▢ THE ▢

PROFESSIONAL IMAGE

The Total Program for Marketing Yourself Visually—
by America's Top Corporate Image Consultant

SUSAN BIXLER

ILLUSTRATED BY LINDA HAAS BALIKO
PHOTOGRAPHS BY KERRY HACKNEY

A Perigee Book

Perigee Books
are published by
The Putnam Publishing Group
200 Madison Avenue
New York, NY 10016

Hair on Models by Charles Corley of Indulgence
Makeup on Models by Ron Guardio

Design by Lynn Braswell

Library of Congress Cataloging in Publication Data

Bixler, Susan
The professional image.

Reprint. Originally published: New York : Putnam,
c1984.
1. Clothing and dress.   2. Fashion.   3. Nonverbal
communication (Psychology)   4. Etiquette.   I. Title.
TT507.B55   1985   646'.3   84-18917
ISBN 0-399-51115-6 (pbk.)

Printed in the United States of America

4   5   6   7   8   9   10

□ THE PROFESSIONAL IMAGE □

To José
My Husband

We belong with each other.

□ ACKNOWLEDGMENTS □

No book is ever written through the efforts of one person. Although many people were a part of this project, there are five very special people who assisted significantly in the publishing of this book.

Susan Percy made a tremendous contribution through her editing and preparation of the manuscript. What could have been a chore was turned into a pleasure by her talent and sense of humor.

Lynne Henderson, Ginger Deans and Susan Trammell, my three associates at The Professional Image, Inc., gave me good, solid advice and went the extra mile in helping with the illustration and photography work.

Judy Linden, my editor, deserves a very special thanks for her clear-headed direction and genuine enthusiasm.

□ CONTENTS □

FOREWORD   15

APPEARANCES DO COUNT   17
HOW WE COMMUNICATE NONVERBALLY ▪ A REASON
TO BE OVERLOOKED ▪ CULTURAL DIFFERENCES ▪
A MEASURING STICK IN EVERY SOCIETY ▪ VISUAL
INTEGRITY ▪ WHY UNPROFESSIONAL?

1 □ WARDROBE: THE FIRST STEP TO YOUR
PROFESSIONAL IMAGE   25
COMPUTER DRESSING ▪ DRESSING FOR YOUR AUDIENCE ▪
SMART CHOICES ▪ MANIPULATING YOUR APPEARANCE ▪
GETTING PAID FOR LOOKING THE PART

2 □ NOT RIGHT OR WRONG BUT APPROPRIATE   32
REGIONAL DIFFERENCES ▪ INDUSTRY DIFFERENCES ▪
CLIMATE CONSIDERATIONS ▪ DIFFERENT ADAPTATIONS ▪
CLASSICS IN THE CLOSET ▪ REFLECTIONS OF LIFESTYLES ▪
THE BENEFITS OF CLASSIC DRESSING

3 ☐ YOUR CLOTHING AS AN INVESTMENT   40
DEVELOPING A PLAN ▪ FEWER ITEMS OF BETTER QUALITY ▪
USING PAST MISTAKES

4 ☐ PLAN YOUR SHOPPING AND SHOP YOUR PLAN   50
CHARTING YOUR COURSE ▪ SAMPLE MAN'S BASIC WARDROBE
▪ SAMPLE WOMAN'S BASIC WARDROBE ▪ SHOPPING ▪ TO THE
DRESSING ROOM ▪ CATALOG SHOPPING

5 ☐ FABRIC: IF IT LOOKS GOOD, WEAR IT   62
FEAR OF POLYESTER ▪ NATURAL FIBERS ▪ MAN-MADE FABRICS

6 ☐ COLOR: THE GOOD, THE BAD, AND
THE NOT SO GOOD   71
COLOR AND EMOTIONS ▪ BASIC WARDROBE COLORS ▪
CONTRASTING AND ACCENT COLORS ▪ PATTERNS

7 ☐ CAMOUFLAGING FIGURE PROBLEMS   82
PROPORTION DRESSING FOR MEN ▪ PROPORTION DRESSING
FOR WOMEN

8 ☐ TINKER, TAILOR, CLEANER: ALTERATIONS AND
CLOTHING CARE   99
YOU AND THE TAILOR ▪ YOU AND THE SEAMSTRESS ▪
ATTENTION TO DETAILS ▪ RESTYLING ▪ CARING FOR YOUR
CLOTHES ▪ SPECIAL CAVEATS

9 ☐ FOR MEN: HOW TO BUY A SUIT   111
HOW MANY AND WHAT KIND ▪ STYLING ▪ FITTING THE SUIT ▪
DETAILING

10 ☐ AND THE SHIRTS AND TIES   122
IF THE SHIRT FITS . . . ▪ COLOR AND STYLE ▪ CUSTOM-MADE
SHIRTS ▪ TIES

11 ☐ LITTLE THINGS MEAN A LOT: ACCESSORIES
FOR MEN   132
UMBRELLAS ▪ BRIEFCASES ▪ SHOES ▪ SOCKS ▪ BELTS ▪
COATS ▪ GLOVES, MUFFLERS ▪ HATS ▪ JEWELRY ▪
HANDKERCHIEFS AND POCKET SCARVES ▪ WALLETS

12 ☐ LOOKING GOOD: MEN'S HAIR AND SKIN CARE   141
FACIAL HAIR ▪ EYEBROWS ▪ NASAL HAIR ▪ MEN'S HAIR STYLES ▪
RECEDING HAIRLINES AND BALDNESS ▪ SKIN CARE

13 ☐ FOR WOMEN: HOW TO BUY A SUIT   148
SUIT JACKETS ▪ CLASSIC SKIRTS ▪ THE KEY ELEMENTS ▪
STYLING DETAILS ▪ CHECKING THE FIT ▪ IT'S A CONSTANT

14 ☐ THE NEXT STEP: DRESSES, BLOUSES,
AND SWEATERS   163
DRESSES FOR COMFORT ▪ BLOUSES: YOUR MOST VERSATILE
ACCESSORY ▪ SWEATERS: AN APPROPRIATE ALTERNATIVE

15 ☐ THE FINE TUNING: WOMEN'S ACCESSORIES   172
SHOES ▪ HOSIERY ▪ SCARVES ▪ JEWELRY ▪ BELTS ▪
RAINCOATS AND TOPCOATS ▪ GLOVES AND MUFFLERS ▪
HATS ▪ FOUL-WEATHER GEAR ▪ PURSES AND BRIEFCASES

16 ☐ TAKING IT FROM THE TOP: WOMEN'S HAIR CARE   182
SHAMPOOING ▪ CONDITIONERS ▪ SELECTING A STYLIST ▪ COLOR
▪ PERMANENTS

17 ☐ PUTTING YOUR BEST FACE FORWARD: WOMEN'S
SKIN CARE AND MAKEUP GUIDE   190
SKIN TYPES ▪ SOAPS AND CLEANSERS ▪ ACNE ▪ SUN AND SKIN
CARE ▪ HYPO-ALLERGENIC COSMETICS ▪ MAKEUP

18 ☐ THE FINAL TOUCHES: GROOMING DETAILS FOR
MEN AND WOMEN   203
   YOUR PEARLY WHITES ▪ HANDS AND NAILS ▪ FRAGRANCE ▪
   DEODORANTS

19 ☐ BODY LANGUAGE IN THE BUSINESS WORLD   209
   INVOLVING OTHERS ▪ WORDS VERSUS DEEDS ▪ MAKING IT
   WORK FOR YOU ▪ DANGER ZONES ▪ UNDERSTANDING THE
   IMPORTANCE OF BODY LANGUAGE

20 ☐ ENTRANCE AND CARRIAGE   215
   "MAKING AN ENTRANCE" ▪ THE WRONG WAY ▪ THE EFFECTIVE
   ENTRANCE ▪ WHEN THE WORST HAPPENS

21 ☐ SHAKING HANDS   221
   A FAIR SHAKE FOR WOMEN ▪ TECHNIQUES ▪ THE LAST
   PHYSICAL CONTACT

22 ☐ MAKING EYE CONTACT   228
   USING EYE CONTACT FOR CONTROL ▪ SINCERE AGREEMENT

23 ☐ BODY POSITIONING: CLOSE ENCOUNTERS   233
   TOUCHING ▪ MEETINGS ▪ POWER POSITIONING ▪ READING YOUR
   AUDIENCE ▪ FLIRTING ▪ SENDING AND RECEIVING MESSAGES

24 ☐ MINDING YOUR P'S AND Q'S: CORPORATE
ETIQUETTE   243
   SMOKING ▪ OPENING DOORS AND HOLDING COATS ▪ PICKING UP
   THE CHECK ▪ TELEPHONE ETIQUETTE

25 ☐ THE WAITING GAME: PROFESSIONALISM DURING
PREGNANCY   248
   CHOOSING YOUR MATERNITY WARDROBE ▪ ACCESSORIES ▪ IN-
   UNDERPINNINGS ▪ HAIR AND MAKEUP ▪ BODY LANGUAGE
   DURING PREGNANCY ▪ ANNOUNCING YOUR PREGNANCY

26 ☐ FIRST IMPRESSIONS: YOUR INTERVIEW IMAGE   257
DRESS THE PART ▪ PLAN AHEAD ▪ BE PREPARED ▪ BEFORE THE
INTERVIEW ▪ DURING THE INTERVIEW

27 ☐ SPECIAL IMAGES FOR SPECIAL OCCASIONS   267
THE BUSINESS ''SOCIAL'' FUNCTION ▪ YOUR PROFESSIONAL
PHOTOGRAPH ▪ TELEVISION APPEARANCES ▪ SPEAKING
ENGAGEMENTS

APPENDIX   279
WARDROBE INVENTORY FOR WOMEN ▪ WARDROBE INVENTORY
FOR MEN

□ THE PROFESSIONAL IMAGE □

□ FOREWORD □

By the time I was in the sixth grade, I was six feet tall. I towered over all my classmates, the teacher, and the principal. It was a rather miserable time in my life because I had always dreamed of being a five-foot-tall cheerleader. I stooped over, slouched, and sat down as much as I could.

In desperation, I inquired into surgical procedures to shorten my legs and drugs to stop my pituitary gland from doing any more damage. I was so busy worrying about my height that I paid very little attention to the other parts of my appearance that had the potential to be changed.

Finally, at some point in my teenage years, I came to the obvious conclusion that no matter what, I was destined to stay six feet tall. Stooping, shuffling, and generally trying to disguise my height only made me look even more self-conscious. Although my height was not a variable, I finally realized that there were a number of variables that could be changed, like my hair, skin, clothing, and even my carriage. So I began to work on them.

About ten years later, I went to work for Bonne Bell cosmetics as a promotional director. My job required me to travel throughout the United States and teach the promotional people whom I hired how to apply makeup. As I observed the makeup demonstrations going on in the department stores, I was struck by one continuing phenomenon! A little paint, properly applied on a woman's face, gave her an extraordinary dose of self-confidence. This didn't happen only with the dramatic cases; it occurred with nearly every woman who sat down and spent ten minutes with cosmetics.

It began to dawn on me that if I could expand this idea, and include hair care, clothing, and even body language—all integral parts of the way these women projected visually—as well as information for men, I would have a very valid concept to sell to corporations.

I accepted a teaching position at the Fashion Institute of Atlanta and began to research my theories. I started a weekly newspaper column on image and incorporated my seminar company, The Professional Image. Because no one ever wants to be a first client, it was tough going initially. But a Marriott franchise owner in Cleveland, Ohio, Boykin Management, took a chance. Since those days, I have spoken to thousands of men and women about their image potential and its critical impact on their professional lives—all based on my ten years in the image-making marketplace.

Whether or not you consider yourself a salesperson, every business person sells—because the first thing that ever gets sold is you. Product and company are secondary.

The Professional Image will help you sell yourself by illustrating the power of visual projection. It is more than a wardrobe guide. This book also includes all aspects of body language, because a fishy handshake and lack of eye contact will quickly dilute the most professional outfit.

Your total appearance says more about you than any verbal message you deliver. This book will help you develop your most effective professional image.

—Susan Bixler

□ APPEARANCES DO COUNT □

If something on the cover of this book enticed you to pick it up, you are one of the millions of Americans who make decisions based on appearances. It is a fact of life that we often judge books by their covers or people by their appearances. Most of us claim to do neither, but we are guilty on both counts. Although people should be judged by their innate worth, it is often a first impression that determines whether someone will stick around long enough to let you reveal it.

If you doubt that people believe what they see, try this experiment the next time you have the opportunity to speak to a group. Ask everyone to make a circle with the thumb and index finger and then place this circle on the *chin*. As you make the request, place your thumb-and-finger circle on your *cheek*. Now look around the room. Most will have followed your visual example, relying more on what they saw than on what they heard. They will have put their little "circle" on their *cheek*. The visual signal will prove more potent than the verbal one. The childhood game of "Simon Says" still lives in the grownup world.

17

HOW WE COMMUNICATE NONVERBALLY

In this country, fifty-five percent of what we believe about one another—whether or not a person is well-educated, intelligent, competent, important, prosperous—is based on our observation and interpretation of nonverbal signals. These are communicated visually and consist of two major components, wardrobe and body language. Each breaks down into more specific categories:

NONVERBAL COMMUNICATION

Wardrobe Development	*Body Language*
CLOTHING	ENTRANCES
ACCESSORIES	HANDSHAKES
HAIR CARE	EYE CONTACT
SKIN CARE	TERRITORY
GROOMING	POSITIONING

Wardrobe actually encompasses much more than clothing. It includes all the peripheral elements of appearance—accessories, hair care, skin care, makeup, and specific elements of grooming. Carefully put together they will project an individual as businesslike, as one who possesses credibility, efficiency, clout, stability, and a sense of personal style.

Haphazardly ordered, they will communicate a very different picture: that of someone who is frivolous, apologetic, lacking confidence, and displaying faddish bad taste. This adds up to a look that won't work in business.

Body language is the other important component of the visual image we project. This includes the information transmitted by eye contact, the way one walks into a room or shakes hands. Personal mannerisms like nodding, nail-biting, hair-twisting and lip-chewing are part of our body language, as are territory or space considerations and even the way we position ourselves among others.

A REASON TO BE OVERLOOKED

American life, particularly American business life, is fast-paced and impatient; time is money. Therefore, anything that saves time has considerable value. If personnel directors, for instance, can find some efficient means of narrowing down a field of a dozen job applicants, rather than spending one hour with each candidate, they will use it. And they do. They look for visual clues to give an indication of a candidate's abilities and qualifications. ("Tell the man in the white socks that the position has been filled." Or "Tell the woman biting her fingernails we have no openings.")

Personnel directors quite literally "look over" the candidates and search for signals that will tell them who is poorly prepared, has the wrong attitude, or has the wrong background. In fact, most recruiters are looking, at least initially, for reasons to eliminate potential employees, especially in periods of high unemployment. They are in a position to be selective and they are.

Thus, the man who shows up in a lime green polyester blazer with a pair of brown "puddlejumpers" may never get a chance to show off his Phi Beta Kappa intelligence. A woman who wears a yellow flouncy dress won't be asked about her MBA. The prospective employer is likely to be turned off by their appearances and to assume, rightly or wrongly, that someone who has not mastered the seemingly simple art of presenting himself or herself professionally has probably not mastered the more complicated arts of practicing law or selling software.

CULTURAL DIFFERENCES

Making judgments and assessments based on external signs is not peculiar to our American culture. Most societies, ancient or modern, have developed some system of measuring and evaluating status among their members. An individual's place in the hierarchy is often signaled by some outward badge—military insignia, for instance. As another example, modern-day Saudi Arabians tend to signal their wealth and importance by wearing as much jewelry as they can to establish their rank. Their evaluation system thrives on overstatement, rather than on understatement.

In Britain, the signal is a verbal one. The accent, intonation, use of vocabulary, even the length of sentences bespeak one's birth and position—much more so than clothing or body language.

The Smithsonian Institution in Washington, D.C., owns a remarkable mural entitled "Modifications of the Soft Tissue." It shows men and women in all parts of the world, from ancient to modern times. Each group displays some type of abnormal change that was considered attractive, desirable, or prestigious within its particular culture.

The bound, crippled feet or "golden lilies" of the Chinese women indicated that they were unable to perform manual labor and were, therefore, members of the elite leisure class. They were prized for their "decorative" value. Elaborate scarifications on the backs of young men from New Guinea were visible signs of their passage into manhood. The cone-shaped heads of inhabitants of the Congo area of Africa were produced by wrapping infants' heads tightly.

In Burma and Thailand wives of wealthy men allowed their necks to be stretched by multiple gold bands, to the point that the neck muscles atrophied. To these people, this was physically attractive. If the husbands became angered or displeased and removed the bands, the women's necks would break. These societies set visual standards as an insidious means of control.

Lest we become smug and view these primitive, seemingly brutal practices with a disdainful eye, there is a very obvious parallel with our modern plastic surgery procedures. Breast implants, nose reconstruction, tummy tucks, chin augmentations and hair transplants are all done on perfectly healthy bodies in order to telegraph a "better message" to society.

A MEASURING STICK IN EVERY SOCIETY

Every society has developed a standard against which all its people are measured. Standards vary from culture to culture, and a culture's standards will change to reflect new values and lifestyles, and even current events.

Over one hundred years ago wealthy Victorians wore delicate high-necked attire that was easily soiled. It covered most of the body and echoed their strict moral code and generally nonphysical lifestyle. In contrast, the American West of this same period saw rough-riding cowboys wearing leather pants and pioneer women in loose, full skirts made of sturdy homespun. Their choices were dictated by their very different geographical and social environments.

Similar comparisons are evident for today's business person, although they are not as dramatic. A big city banker does not wear the same attire as one who lives in a small town. It's not necessary, practical, or correct for one to imitate the other's choice of garments. An urban banker probably conducts business in a conference room; a rural banker may sell his services in a farmhouse kitchen. There is an appropriate business attire for each.

VISUAL INTEGRITY

A visual presence must have a certain amount of integrity and consistency. Clothes alone won't do the trick. Scarlett O'Hara discovered this when she tried to convince Rhett Butler she was still a woman of means. Visiting him in jail, dressed in an elegant gown made from old draperies, Scarlett almost succeeded with her charade, but her rough, calloused hands belied her finery.

In the same sense a business person who tries to upgrade his appearance without an understanding of the whole picture may produce instead an air of phoniness. One good suit does not carry the day. The shirt or blouse, shoes, carriage and handshake all play a major role and must work together to convey a message of genuine professionalism. Lack of attention to important details can negate the entire effort.

Perhaps because this country has long been a land of opportunity, we have devised a system for projecting a positive presence that anyone can master within a reasonable time. The system is based not on wealth or birth, but on effective nonverbal communication. All that's necessary is to learn the rules and techniques of visual projection and make a sustained effort to integrate them into your business or professional sphere. Although educational credentials and good work experience take many years to accumulate, building a professional image requires a relatively small investment of time and money. *Looking professional is a skill that can be mastered by anyone who wants to learn it.*

WHY UNPROFESSIONAL?

Why don't people project themselves professionally? Why do they create a negative impression that cripples their career efforts?

Some people think of clothing simply as a means of hiding their nakedness or keeping themselves warm in the winter.

Others don't understand how to dress for the corporate world. Young people who have spent their last sixteen years in school, whose work experience was limited to frying hamburgers in fast-food restaurants, may not have had the opportunity to develop ideas on style, taste, and appropriateness.

It was not until 1956 that white-collar workers outnumbered blue-collar workers in America. Over two decades later women outnumbered men in the work force. The man whose father worked in a blue-collar job and the woman whose mother stayed at home lacked role models who could have helped them develop a sense of style that fits the corporate world.

Growing up, many women devoted much time and effort to trying to appear fashionable and appealing to men. They searched for an identity through clothes. Unfortunately, this is not the best preparation for building a business wardrobe.

There are other reasons why individuals project overstated images. People who come from poor backgrounds often resort to overkill when they are finally able to afford the material items they were denied as children. Dolly Parton admits to this. She wears Barbie Doll wigs, false eyelashes, and flashy, glittery clothes because those were all things she longed for but couldn't have as a youngster. Sammy Davis, Jr., wears pounds of gold chains and rings on every finger because now he can afford to do so.

Often people get locked into a particular look and fail to let go of it because they don't want to part with a particular time in their lives. They associate their look with their good memories. Thus you see middle-aged business women wearing the same teased and lacquered hair styles they had when their husbands proposed marriage, and younger women who cling to their Farrah Fawcett hairdos because that's what worked on prom night. Or you find men in business who really should put their flat-top haircuts into mothballs along with their old military fatigues.

Few people want to present a poor image. Ironically, most of us are better able to recognize someone else's clothing mistakes than our own. Yet there is a small minority who know they look terrible and simply don't care. It is often shocking to meet the owners or founders of very successful high technology firms because their business success seems to be in direct *disproportion* to the success of their appearance.

Certainly each of us can come up with an example of someone who has succeeded in spite of a poor image: the president of a top-notch insurance company who looks like a janitor, the computer genius who looks like a pile of dirty clothes. Sometimes these people have positions that require little public contact; sometimes they were just lucky.

Their sloppiness conveys the suggestion that they have loftier things with which to occupy themselves. They feel that paying too much attention to dress or appearance is frivolous. This tiny minority has succeeded despite a lack of professionalism in dress. These people's highly recognized gifts were such an important contribution to business that they outshone any lack of sensitivity to appearance. (Remember the goofy guy who won the science fair at your high school and now runs an electronics conglomerate?)

Most of us, though, are not so fortunate or so gifted; we need every advantage we can get—especially one as attainable as visual presence. So I often wonder how much more quickly these people would have achieved their rewards if they had learned the technique of marketing themselves visually.

The direction in which American business is moving is going to make attention to dress even more important in the future. Eighty percent of the workforce dresses in some type of business attire other than uniforms and blue-collar clothes. Factory jobs are rapidly becoming automated. Indeed, as the "information revolution" presses on, professional image will take on added importance.

Both wardrobe and body language "speak" more eloquently about you than anything you actually say. How you dress and how you move: these things taken together are your visual presence. It is up to you whether that image works for you or against you.

1

WARDROBE: THE FIRST STEP TO YOUR PROFESSIONAL IMAGE

Department store Santas, fire fighters and mail carriers have few crucial decisions to make about what to wear on the job. But many business people begin their decision-making each morning at seven o'clock standing in front of their closets and selecting their attire for the day. It's not always an easy choice. The changes in our lives, work places, and attitudes are often reflected in what we put in our closets, and ultimately on our backs.

The last twenty years have seen some dramatic manifestations of change: men with long hair and women with short hair; the no-bra look; the army-surplus-store look; the rise and fall of the woman's pantsuit for business, and the "denimization" of the Western Hemisphere. It was a resolute soul who could resist every new trend.

One of the crucial factors in all of this was the rapid change in the role of women as they became a majority in the workforce and assumed positions of more responsibility within the corporate world. This particular phenomenon caught the fashion industry napping. While the business woman was striving to look like a professional, the fashion industry was trying its best to make her into a gypsy, cowgirl, coquette, or Cinderella.

Fifteen years ago women became frustrated when they looked for conservative business suits. Today, nearly every manufacturer of men's suits also makes the same garments for women.

Men's roles in business actually have changed very little over the past two centuries. This is reflected in the relatively small amount of change in their clothing, particularly among manufacturers that cater to the classic look. Brooks Brothers, for example, is still selling many of the same basic styles that it sold when it opened its doors in 1818.

Yet not everyone saw things as clearly as the conservative men's stores. Too many business persons relied upon their own instincts, so the Christmas ties and birthday shirts that came their way showed up at the office, along with a whole range of other unfortunate personal choices. Pinstriped shirts that resembled pajamas, sherbet-colored suits, jumbo ties that all but glowed in the dark, and leisure suits that should have been accorded a decent burial were all mixed and mismatched with abandon. Clearly, there was a need for someone or something to make some sense out of all the clothing chaos.

COMPUTER DRESSING

In the early seventies the "science" of business dress was born. The emergence of "computer" dressing brought the unofficial uniform look, which was very similar for both men and women: a navy suit with a long-sleeved white shirt. It was not bad as a first concept but it overlooked individual jobs, personalities, and especially personal taste. "Formula" dressing was just plain boring.

The corporate uniform may have been a necessary first step toward an accepted professional look, but it was a monotonous one. It became obvious that no single look could successfully be pasted on everyone, like one set of cut-out clothes on millions of paper dolls. Clearly, a professional image could not overlook individuality.

Fortunately, the eighties have seen the softening of the business uniform, especially for women, most of whom simply will not be bullied into wearing a dark, tailored suit every single day. Women are secure enough to wear dresses with and without jackets. Men, too, have learned that a navy-blue three-piece suit might be an excellent wardrobe choice, but it certainly isn't the only one.

The same power uniform actually loses its punch when it is worn every day. It becomes so commonplace that it goes unnoticed. Certainly, consistency in dress is important, but the power uniform—the heavy artillery— is usually best saved for occasions or situations that demand it.

Besides, such a "power" uniform, whether it is a masculine or feminine version, can work against you if it is worn inappropriately. It may intimidate people. After all, professional dress should not serve to make you outshine everyone else, nor to "one-up" a client. *Image is a tool one uses to accomplish an objective.* A casually dressed retail owner in a rural area is not going to be comfortable trying to do business with a power-suited "city slicker."

The clone look is dead—from overexposure. It gave no one an advantage and therefore no one has any reason to mourn its passing.

DRESSING FOR YOUR AUDIENCE

Rita Jenrette may have helped lose the case for her Congressman husband, John, because of her courtroom attire. While he was pleading bankruptcy, she was wearing thousand-dollar designer outfits. His verbal testimony lost credibility because of her visual message. Contrast this to the almost matronly look that high-fashion model Cristina Ferrare adopted when her husband, John De Lorean, faced a long series of court appearances immediately after his narcotics arrest. She was aware of how her image could affect his verdict. So she opted for dark, very simple suits, a short plain hair style and a small amount of makeup and jewelry. She adapted her appearance to her new circumstances and to a different audience.

It was not entirely the weather that prompted former New York City Mayor John Lindsay to shed his suit jacket and tie several years ago when he was trying to win votes in the city's low-income neighborhoods. He was attempting to make himself more appealing to his audience. This principle is exactly what professional dressing is all about.

If your audience is the board of directors, you dress for them. If it's the guys at the loading dock, you take off your jacket, roll up your sleeves, and shed your tie or scarf. Varying your wardrobe will vary your impact and serve you better. And remember that every outfit delivers a message.

A woman who shows up for a job interview in a lemon-colored Ultrasuede suit looks as though she should be lunching at the country club, not launching a career. A man who shows up for the same interview in a shiny polyester suit, a short wide tie, and a sweater vest does not appear to be taking the interview seriously.

The woman is saying that she doesn't really need to work, that she is a dilettante looking for something to do between tennis matches. The man's casual look is saying that the job is unimportant.

Good business people are always conscious of the immediate impression they make with their attire. A man trying to sell a small computer to the guy who owns the corner Shell station is probably going to be making his sales presentation while the prospective buyer is in greasy overalls. An aware salesperson would feel foolish standing there in a three-piece suit clutching an attaché case. The gas station owner would feel intimidated. A sensitivity to the selling situation means that the salesperson will shed his coat, roll up his sleeves and loosen his tie before strolling into the station. However, if his next call is on the vice-president of sales at a Fortune 500 company, the tie is put back into place, and the suit jacket is brushed off and put on.

SMART CHOICES

Appropriate is the key word. And within the appropriate range there are usually sufficient choices available to satisfy yourself, your company, and your customers. When I consult with individuals, I am more successful when I help them determine what works best for them, rather than simply dictating stringent lists of do's and don'ts. For example, a veteran engineer for a computer company was promoted to head of his division. He wanted some help with his wardrobe and needed an opinion about his nicely trimmed beard. Although it was thick and well groomed, I had some reservations. I asked to see the people in his department and found that most of the other men had beards, too. But I advised my client to shave off his so that he wouldn't look like "one of the guys." He needed a separate, more corporate identity. The engineer looked handsome in a beard, but his career opportunities and future advancement were more enhanced when he was clean-shaven.

Similarly, a female branch manager for a small bank wanted to know whether it was all right to wear a blond wig on days that her hair looked dirty. Instead of simply telling her to wash her hair more often, I asked her the same question that I put to the engineer: "Will it help or hinder your career advancement?" She made the decision to adopt a simpler hair style that would be easier to maintain and would eliminate the need for the wig.

Each of us has the opportunity to develop whatever type of visual message we wish to send to our bosses, coworkers and clients. It is possible to dress above or below our actual level in business. Many ambitious young people dress above their positions, consciously trying to create the impression that they are destined for better things. If the image is backed up by ability, they usually are.

If you work for a large corporation, pay attention to the way the successful employees dress. You will probably notice that people's dress improves as their importance within the company increases—it rarely goes in the other direction. Top-level management people tend to look successful. You would not often mistake a junior clerk for a senior vice-president; if you did, that might well indicate the clerk was on the way up or the vice-president on the way down.

On the other hand, our office received a call when a fast-tracked woman was promoted to a higher level and gradually began turning in her conservative skirted suits for a fashionable bangled bracelet look. Her supervisor called our offices to request an individual wardrobe consultation. After a discussion, it was apparent that the woman knew how to dress professionally. She was simply electing not to do so. This newly promoted woman was indicating visually that her present position was as high as she wanted to go. She was intentionally, or perhaps unintentionally, telling the company not to consider her for future promotions.

MANIPULATING YOUR APPEARANCE

Occasionally a situation demands dressing down. A successful Southeastern developer finds it works to his advantage, in some instances, to dress the part of the "good old boy," especially when he is outside the corporate limits of Atlanta and Birmingham. His clients are then farmers or builders wearing hard hats. We suggested that he not wear blue jeans and boots—but no banker's pinstripe either. In this situation, a navy blazer, open-collared, button-down shirt and a pair of pressed khaki pants work nicely.

A female journalist says it sometimes works to her advantage to be understated, depending on the person she is interviewing. In her "power" costume—dark suit and tailored blouse—she notices that certain people tend to be more cautious about what they say; dressed more casually—a dirndl skirt and a well-tailored business sweater—she puts people more at ease and they often tell her more than they initially intended. But it is her audience that determines her attire. When she spoke at a monthly meeting of female journalists, she wore a much stronger outfit.

By manipulating our clothing and appearance, we are using visual impact to its best advantage. We can ascribe an importance or lack of importance to ourselves, and give a strong visual suggestion of our background, education, and future prospects.

GETTING PAID FOR LOOKING THE PART

Research indicates that it is financially beneficial to present a dynamic, well-polished image in business. Funded by the Clairol Corporation, psychologist Dr. Judith Waters from Fairleigh Dickinson University researched the impact an effective business appearance has on a starting salary. She sent out a large number of "before" and "after" photographs and identical resumes to more than a thousand companies. No company received both a "before" and "after" picture. Each was asked to determine a starting salary.

The results were amazing. They indicated an initial salary of eight to twenty percent higher as the result of upgrading a mediocre business appearance to one that is crisp and effective.

Employers are quite willing to pay more for people who already look the part. There is the inference that employees who care about themselves will care about their jobs.

If employees are already projecting an image of professionalism through their dress, that's one less thing—and a potentially unpleasant thing—that the firm has to worry about. It also leaves more time for instructing the employee on product information and company procedure, and for other essential training.

American businesses and corporations will generally reward, through increased salary and promotions, those professionals who project effectively. A well-polished image gives you a genuine competitive edge and stamps you as someone on the way up.

2

NOT RIGHT OR WRONG BUT APPROPRIATE

There is nothing wrong with a frilly white dress or a comfortable corduroy jacket with leather patches on the elbow. Each, if it fits well and looks good, may be an important addition to a wardrobe. However, neither garment belongs in the office. Nor, by the same token, does a three-piece pin-striped suit belong at the beach. Every outfit has a definite "on-the-job" or "off-the-job" look.

In business dressing, it is not a matter of what is right or wrong; what counts is whether the clothes are appropriate or inappropriate. What is appropriate can vary greatly from one region of the country to another, from one industry to another, from one climate to another.

REGIONAL DIFFERENCES

In Texas and other Western states where a lot of business is transacted outdoors, savvy businessmen can wear well-polished, well-heeled cowboy boots with their business suits. The general business environment of the West often makes cowboy boots appropriate. But if they are worn outside their region, it could be suicidal.

During one of our Professional Image workshops held on the East Coast, we had two businessmen who had been transferred east from South Dakota. They both had beards, well-polished cowboy boots and Western-styled suits; and they looked like two ducks out of water. Knowing that their appearance was going to cause them a lot of grief on the job, they opted for mustaches, black slip-on shoes and more classically styled suits. But they took their cowboy boots with them every time they went back West on business.

Dress standards are more casual in Florida than Pennsylvania. Something that works in Tampa—brighter colors, slightly larger prints, for instance—would not work in Philadelphia. Even within the state of Florida, the business people in Tampa dress more conservatively than those in Fort Lauderdale. The sophistication of a region and cultural preferences play a great part in the selection of appropriate business dress.

INDUSTRY DIFFERENCES

Bankers, stockbrokers, and insurance people dress more conservatively than the creative director for an ad agency. The former group is required to convey an image of solid trustworthiness, since they are people who handle other people's money; the latter must present to clients the idea that he or she is "up-to-the-minute" and on the cutting edge of what is new and in fashion.

People who are expected to be creative in their jobs—artists, designers, and musicians—are expected, at times, to look creative, even eccentric. People in the entertainment business can and do dress more flamboyantly than those in other fields. Although their objective is the same as that of anyone else in business—to sell themselves and their product—their means of doing it is unique. Someone selling a rock group should not project the same message as someone selling eternal security through life insurance. The more serious and heavyweight the business, the more conservative and serious the clothing.

Yet even in a creative business like advertising or public relations, a client is often investing huge sums of money and wants to feel reassured that he is dealing with competent people. This being the case, it is far wiser to adopt a more conservative style of creative dressing when dealing with corporate clients. The idea is to appear fashionable yet also responsible and stable, not as someone who will be frivolous with a client's money.

CLIMATE CONSIDERATIONS

Climate often dictates particular clothing choices. In Atlanta, tassel loafers and thin-soled slip-ons are perfectly appropriate in most business circles and are worn by lawyers, stockbrokers, and conservative salesmen. They are lighter shoes, well suited to a warmer climate.

But the same shoes in Boston are too informal; a wing tip is a better choice. The heavier-soled and more substantial shoe is better in colder and snowier weather. A tassel loafer or an Italian leather slip-on would last two weeks in the slush.

If you're not comfortable, you are not going to be at your best. The seersucker suit you don in New Orleans for your plane trip to Seattle in October will look and feel much too light once you reach your destination. A gray flannel suit is a smart choice in Cleveland and a hot mistake in Texas. A fur coat for a woman is only appropriate where it is actually needed for warmth: New York . . . yes, Miami . . . no. A man, even in Fairbanks, Alaska, should shy away from fur entirely unless it lines his plain wool overcoat.

Yet even in these cold climates, furs ought to be worn selectively. A fur coat is an attention-getter. Some of the people a woman meets when she is wearing her full-length coyote may be green with envy; others may be offended by the idea of killing animals for personal adornment. Neither arousing jealousy nor appearing insensitive is likely to start you off on your best business foot, especially if you are trying to do business with the city zoo, the Society for the Prevention of Cruelty to Animals or an antipoverty organization.

Save the fur for cold days when you are certain clients will understand your choice of attire, and for nonbusiness occasions.

DIFFERENT ADAPTATIONS

There are probably several different styles you will want to include in your wardrobe, all within the range of what is professionally appropriate, so that you feel comfortable with the climate, your city, and your industry.

A salesperson might spend Monday in the office catching up on phone work and paperwork. Here a more casual look is fine. Tuesday and Wednesday is cold-calling on new office complexes, so visual presence needs to be much stronger and more businesslike yet not intimidating. Thursday is a formal presentation to a new group of marketing directors, so a dose of visual intimidation is probably going to bolster self-confidence. Friday calls for a friendlier version of the professional look, because that day is for servicing long-time accounts.

Such a varied schedule requires flexibility in dress. Yet most of us lack the time and money to purchase several different business wardrobes. We need a simpler and more economical answer than that. Fortunately the answer to the whole dilemma of business dressing is amazingly simple: think classic.

CLASSICS IN THE CLOSET

Classics are so called because their cut, styling, and detailing defy fads and the changing dictates of the fashion industry. Classics don't change every season; they have no need to. A man's suit with three-inch lapels, natural shoulders, and straight-legged trousers will look correct year after year. A woman's suit in an easily accessorized color, with a permanent hemline and slightly padded shoulders, will not date itself.

In contrast, a fad is a short-lived, "hot" item that has a brief and often very intense acceptance, then burns itself out in six months. But something new that catches on and gains broader acceptance, mostly because it is flattering on most people, transcends faddishness and escalates to a trend.

Bell-bottom pants, vinyl go-go boots, slit skirts, and the metallic look were fads. However, unstructured jackets, pleated pants, and paisley ties have stayed around for quite a while and have become trends. Even the button-down shirt, which was originally introduced in the early 1900s, was once brand new and potentially a fad. But scores of years later it still graces the wardrobes of many business men and women.

Some trendy items try for a comeback every few years, often with a new name and a cut just different enough from its previous incarnation to allow the old to be discarded for the fashionable new. Many times we will hold on to a dated item, knowing it will come back into style, only to find out that an important detail has been added or subtracted, which makes our cedar-chest garment obsolete.

The divided skirt is an example of this. It has been around the block several times as gaucho pants, culottes, and the split skirt, each with a different look, but none classic enough to endure. The women who have invested in any of these variations for business have found them pushed to the back of the closet in a very short time.

The fads in your closet (Nehru jackets, slit-up-the-side skirts, backless "streetwalker" shoes) will rust-out, but the classics will live on and on, wearing out only after years of continued use. Classically cut clothes are time-honored styles that never date. Not only are they timeless but they are also always correct for business.

Fashion designers periodically rediscover classic styling and launch it as though it had just been invented; other years, classics are relegated to a lower fashion rung. The reason is simple. The fashion industry will not make money unless it introduces something new and different, so it can't perennially feature the classics.

Left to our own devices, most of us would choose garments that flatter our bodies, making us look—and therefore feel—good. But too many fashion designers are determined to give us only outfits that make us look twenty pounds heavier and twelve inches wider. (It is no accident that top fashion models are toothpick-thin: no one else can wear some of the ridiculous designs that come off the drawing boards of the avante garde designers. Remember how we looked in baggy jeans?)

Undeniably, change is healthy. But when clothing becomes confusing and prohibitively expensive, it should be rejected. Permanent guidelines, not rigid dicta, are what serve the business person best.

REFLECTIONS OF LIFESTYLES

Men's clothing has remained more constant than women's, avoiding the wide swings of the pendulum. This reflects men's more static position in our society. Except for a short slip into the insanity of the sixties, conservative men's stores have stayed with the standards they set years ago. Part of the reason for this is that men don't demand the fashion changes that women do.

But women, finally, are catching on to the advantages of classic clothing, and demanding some invariables of their own—such as permanent hemlines, styling that won't date for at least five years, and colors and fabrics that are transitional. Who, after all, has the money or the time to start from scratch every two years?

Despite its longevity, classic clothing is not boring—far from it. A classically styled suit always has many more possibilities than a very trendy style. A faddish suit has

Remember the sixties look?

to be worn always as a unit, usually with only one set of accessories.

A faddish man's suit will generally take only a certain type of tie and a very specific shirt. A conservative shoe like a wing tip will look ridiculously heavy with it. Extremely fashionable suits are generally cut for very slim men with not one extra inch in the waist, and that eliminates most members of the male population, who gain and lose the same five pounds two or three times a year.

The individual pieces of an extremely high-fashion woman's suit cannot be worn as separates. The jacket usually will go with nothing else and the cut of the skirt will generally make it look odd without the jacket. Contrasting piping means it will take a very limited number of blouses, possibly just one.

It is impossible to update a fad suit with new accessories. The standard width three-inch tie will look out of place on a five-inch, wide-lapeled, one-season suit. New additions of scarves, jewelry, and interesting blouses are hopeless on a very stylized, quickly dated woman's suit. A fad suit is meant to be worn one way and one way only. Any attempt to update it so you can wear it for another year usually falls flat.

THE BENEFITS OF CLASSIC DRESSING

Classic clothes are always appropriate business attire; they can be accessorized to work in any business or profession. They can look simple and conservative for insurance and banking or can be given a more fashionable look for publishing and retailing.

Classic styles have the advantage of flattering most figure types, especially those that are slightly overweight or lack perfect proportions. Classic cuts drop from the natural shoulder and the natural waistline. They skim over figure problems.

It is not unusual to take an overweight man or woman out of a bulky, layered look or a too-small and too-tight look and, with properly fitted classic clothes, help him or her "lose" ten or twenty pounds. Paradoxically, thin people will find the classics kindest to their bodies because there are no jarring skirt lines that end above the knee or tightly tapered trouser legs showing off skinny legs.

A closet full of classic clothing is like a portfolio of blue-chip stocks: no risks, no worries, and always a good return on your investment.

3

YOUR CLOTHING AS AN INVESTMENT

Setting up a business is expensive and involves some time-consuming details—many of them related to "image." A high-priced specialty store can't look like a used-car lot and a BMW dealership can't run ads that look like discount grocery store come-ons.

Most people understand that the way their business "looks" is worth the time and effort spent on choosing furniture, selecting stationery, or packaging a product to make it attractive to the consumer. These things are recognized as important and worthy of an appropriate dollar investment.

But the first thing that ever gets sold is the salesperson. Product always comes second, so it is surprising how many business people balk at devoting any resources to packaging themselves dynamically. Employees are living, breathing extensions of a company. They are the very best advertisements.

Selecting a wardrobe cannot be done with two hundred dollars and a lunch hour. It is an important part of your business and should be treated as such. Acquiring an appropriate professional wardrobe involves the same kind of research, planning, and commitment you devote to any other aspect of your career. Most financial investments are analyzed very carefully. Yet the unwise purchases hanging in business people's closets represent thousands of dollars misspent. Since all of us allocate a certain amount of money for our clothing, it makes sense that the money and time we invest in a business wardrobe should be well spent.

DEVELOPING A PLAN

It makes sense to have a plan and to buy the very best quality you can afford for your business wardrobe. These are the garments you will wear the most.

A WORKING PERSON'S TWENTY-FOUR-HOUR DAY USUALLY BREAKS DOWN SOMETHING LIKE THIS:

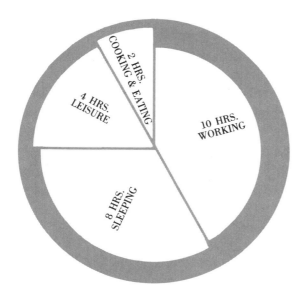

Doesn't it make sense to forgo a hundred-dollar tennis outfit and spend the money where it will be more utilized? Doesn't it make sense to put your money where you put your time?

Another way of viewing the economics of clothing acquisition is to use the *Cost Per Wearing Formula* to see how much your clothes really "cost." This is a concept that has been around for years, and it does provide a graphic illustration of clothing value. Multiply the number of wearings per month *times* the number of months per year the item can be worn *times* the number of years the item will be in your wardrobe. The result is the total number of wearings. Then,

$$\text{cost of item} \div \text{total wearings} = \text{cost per wearing}$$

Let's take a business suit that costs $250. It is a medium-weight wool blend with a hard worsted finish, which means that it can be worn in most climates at least nine months out of the year. It can easily be worn once a week and it is classic enough so that it will look correct for at least four years.

Item One—A wool blend suit for $250.

$$5 \text{ wearings per month} \times 9 \text{ months per year} \times 4 \text{ years} = 180 \text{ wearings}$$
$$\$250 \div 180 \text{ wearings} = \$1.39 \text{ per wearing}$$

Then take the same amount of money and consider the purchase of an evening gown or tuxedo.

Item Two—An evening outfit for $250.

$$1 \text{ wearing per year} \times 4 \text{ years} = 4 \text{ wearings}$$
$$\$250 \div 4 \text{ wearings} = \$62.50 \text{ per wearing}$$

Although a classic men's tuxedo can be worn until it wears out, most women won't wear an evening outfit for four years unless it is a truly stunning classic. No woman wants her red chiffon gown to be the official harbinger of the holiday season.

You can indulge your taste for fads when you are shopping for clothes that don't get worn so often, like evening wear. But put most of your money in your business clothes for a maximum return on your investment.

FEWER ITEMS OF BETTER QUALITY

That quality counts should come as no surprise. It is far more advantageous to have several quality outfits than hordes of cheap-looking items. But most of us have invested in a closet full of errors. Unless someone torches our entire wardrobe, we won't have the opportunity to replace everything. But we can learn from our mistakes.

One well-fitting lightweight wool or wool blend jacket for $150 is a far better investment than two inexpensive polyester jackets for $75 each. Even if the total price is comparable, the value isn't. Wool or wool blend will last much longer and flatter a figure better. It molds to the shape of the body rather than hanging like a cardboard box. Wool will also save money, because it is the longest-lasting of fibers. If it is a lighter-weight wool or wool blend, it can be worn almost year round because it will breathe, unlike one-hundred-percent man-made fibers.

The garments hanging in your closet probably represent an investment of somewhere between one and five thousand dollars. It is amazing how much money we spend on clothes and how little we have to show for it.

I once did an individual consultation with a professional woman who had about four thousand dollars worth of clothing in her closet. That wasn't too surprising. But the surprise came when she realized that two thousand dollars was invested in evening wear and another thousand dollars had been spent on tennis, jogging, and aerobic dancing attire. Only about one quarter, or one thousand dollars, of her clothing expenditure had gone toward the kind of clothes she wears at least ten hours of her day, five days a week. She had only two good suits and two sets of accessories to her name—in contrast to ten different sports outfits and four lavish evening ensembles. No wonder she felt that she had nothing to wear.

In doing individual wardrobe consultations I have found that very often only twenty percent of an individual's wardrobe is wisely purchased; sometimes eighty, even ninety percent of what's filling up a closet represents a waste of money. That leaves a great many bargains that should have been resisted: odd-colored shirts and blouses that never quite worked, trousers and skirts we promised to diet our way into, or fad items that died a mercifully swift death.

When you think of it, ten to twenty percent is a pretty poor return on a large investment. Imagine handing over a thousand dollars to an investment counselor and being satisfied when you get back only two hundred dollars.

USING PAST MISTAKES

It is possible to use these past shopping mistakes to help make future shopping trips more productive. In fact, it's actually fairly easy to pinpoint what went wrong. When we make a shopping mistake, whether it is a twenty-dollar or a two-hundred-dollar one, it is likely that we fell into one of four traps: the Sale Sign Trap, the Designer Label Trap, the In-a-Hurry Trap, or the No-Planning Trap.

THE SALE SIGN TRAP

Normally sane and rational people tend to put their judgment on hold when they are confronted by a sign that says "sale." Indeed, what else but a "clearance" or "reduced fifty percent" sign has the power to turn an ugly yellow blazer into an enchanting one? Only a sale sign can stretch a pair of size 10 pants over a size 12 posterior, or convince us that we can't live without a floral print tie.

The most common reason for making clothing mistakes is that the item was on sale. Not many of us have the fortitude to pass up a great buy. Never mind that the price is already marked up at least one hundred percent over cost, or that the orange-and-green blouse doesn't go with anything you already own. So what if thirteen pairs of short socks on clearance provide twenty-six new opportunities to show off hairy legs. We buy.

I have taken clients shopping and found, to my amazement, that the reduced price tag is often the sole determining factor for deciding that they like something. If the item is a three-hundred-dollar jacket reduced to one hundred dollars, it doesn't matter that the color, fabric, and fit are lacking. Only the vast reduction in price is important.

Finding a great bargain that works is the dream of all shoppers; but fooling yourself into thinking a jacket looks better just because it is reduced seventy percent is a costly mistake. It helps to understand something about retailing, so you understand why items go on sale.

Why a reduction in price? Most clothing stores make their biggest profits early in the season, when prices are highest. At this point the customer is paying not only for the garment itself, but also for the wide selection and the chance to be the first to wear it. As the season wears on, stores mark down the unsold merchandise, perhaps two or three times. They want to make room for the next season's styles. So this summer's fad jacket on sale in late August is not necessarily a bargain, but a classically cut, lightweight beige blazer probably is.

There are other reasons a store might put items on sale. Sometimes the store overorders and simply needs to "move" the surplus merchandise. Sometimes the store stocks an item that is not in demand by its clientele. Thus a store that directs its advertising to the teenybopper crowd but lays in a supply of conservative business suits as a new item might end the season without having sold the units. In that case, the business person who happens to take a teenager shopping and stumbles upon this sale rack may be in luck.

Often a garment is on sale because it was a mistake. The cut is not flattering, the color is last year's introduction, the stitching is uneven, the zipper is broken, there is dirt or a makeup mark on the sleeve. Some of these things spell disaster, but others don't. If the smudge mark is simply dirt a dry cleaning may remove it. If you're handy with a needle you can replace the broken zipper. Simply remember that you will be wearing the garment, not the sale tag.

THE DESIGNER LABEL TRAP

DLS—short for Designer Label Syndrome—can be fatal to a wardrobe. For some reason, there is a premium placed by many people on wearing other people's initials. It offers a kind of security to those who cannot draw it from anything else.

Manufacturers pay designers large licensing fees for the privilege of emblazoning their wares with a famous signature or initials. But if you think that the advertised designer personally creates each item that bears his or her name, then you probably still believe in the Tooth Fairy.

Do you really think that every Pierre Cardin item comes off the drawing board of the designer himself? Or that Gloria Vanderbilt supervises the construction of all the jeans that sport her swan logo? Depending on the merchandise—and the amount of money that changes hands—the designer may discuss some ideas, do a preliminary sketch, or simply give approval. Or someone on the designer's staff may take care of that.

If a garment—designer-approved or not—fits into your clothing plan and you can afford it, then buy it. But first mentally remove the label. Does it still look good? Then after you buy it, physically remove any obvious label. If you are sold on initials, why not use your own?

Three places that designer initials should absolutely be avoided are on ties (where initials only serve to lower the appeal of the garment), on scarves (a very obvious attempt to assert status), and on handbags (too country-club looking).

There was a time when a designer name might have conveyed some sort of cachet. Years ago aspiring maîtres d'hôtel at exclusive European hotels were trained to drape a diner's coat behind the chair in such a way that the label would show. But now that labels and initials are so commonplace,

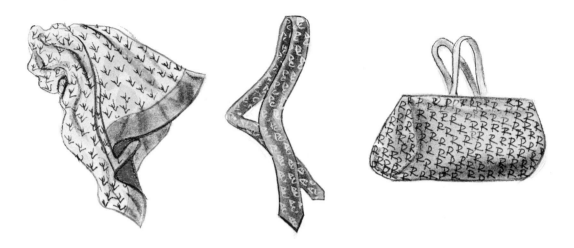

Avoid designer overkill.

the "snob" value has diminished; only the free advertising factor remains. And that benefits the seller, not the buyer.

THE IN-A-HURRY TRAP

Frantic shopping trips are responsible for a great many clothing mistakes. We need an interviewing suit, we need a presentation outfit, we have a client's cocktail party to attend. All that urgency adds up to more mistakes in our closet. The last minute is the worst possible time to shop.

When we are pressed for time, we aren't cautious. We compromise. We lose sight of everything except the fact that we need something to wear. Anything! So what if the sleeves are a little short and there is a button missing, we need it now. So what if the purchase will require a completely new set of accessories. We buy. And one failure leads to another.

It makes a great deal more sense to plan a wardrobe to cover the contingencies and to do our shopping free of pressures. Most of us can make educated guesses about the kind of working and social activities in which we will engage. Besides, it is never a good idea to wear a new, untried outfit on an important occasion. If you're already nervous about an interview, board meeting, or television appearance, you want an "old friend" who promises you no surprises. Wear something you know will be comfortable and correct.

Try out a new outfit on some ordinary day. After all, you don't experiment with a new chocolate mousse recipe the night the boss is coming to dinner; you stick with a proven winner. The same holds true for your clothes. Wear something you can trust if you already have something to be nervous about.

Barney's in New York recognizes the folly of last-minute, desperate shopping. Their slogan is "We want you to select, not settle." That's good advice wherever you shop.

THE NO-PLANNING TRAP

Untold amounts of money are thrown out the window through lack of wardrobe planning. Failing to plan your clothing investment means planning to fail. All of us know the feeling of needing something to wear that sends us running to the nearest shopping mall with no clear idea of what that "something" is.

One woman likens the situation to that of a pioneer going into the woods with a musket determined to bring home dinner. "You know you're going to bag something and bring it home."

In that frame of mind, we are sitting ducks. We have no real idea what is in our closet—or what works and what doesn't. We wander aimlessly around the store, hoping something will catch our eye. And we will play right into the hands of the marketers. Retail stores spend millions of dollars researching the psychology of merchandising, and there is no one the stores would rather see coming through their doors than you—armed with your charge card and a determination to use it no matter what.

That puts you in a vulnerable position. You will tend to gravitate toward whatever is displayed most prominently. It is no accident that "new arrivals" are so visible. These are often items the store will try to entice you to buy on impulse because the color is attractive or because the entire look is put together. And that look is likely to be expensive. All you have to do is charge it, and then figure out when and where you can wear it.

It's the same principle that leads grocery stores to stock the gourmet or exotic foods near the entrance, so they can dazzle you when you first walk in. No grocery store manager with any marketing savvy would put milk and bread near the entrance; you will find them in back of the store. But the hearts of palm, smoked oysters, and French sesame seed crackers are the things they need to "sell" to you.

If you find yourself shopping without any sort of plan you will end up with the clothing equivalent of smoked oysters and hearts of palm—lots of accompaniments but no main course. A clothing plan will give you direction, illuminate "holes" in your present wardrobe, and help you chart your next purchases.

4

PLAN YOUR SHOPPING AND SHOP YOUR PLAN

The best business wardrobes begin with a plan. Just as companies project their income and expenditures, you need to plan specifically how you will invest the next fifty dollars or five hundred dollars or one thousand dollars you spend for your clothing.

Your first step takes you literally into your closet, where you will go through every single item you find there and relegate it to one of four separate piles. The first pile is for the things that are totally useless; the second is for those items that are marginal; the third, and probably the smallest of the piles, is for those items of clothing that you wear regularly—things that you like—and feel comfortable in. The fourth pile is for sportswear and formal wear—simply put those aside and deal with them later. We are focusing now on only your professional clothing.

You may have to be ruthless in your sorting, particularly when you are consigning your mistakes to the "throw-away pile." These are the things you will donate to a charity—taking the appropriate tax deduction, of course. This pile includes clothes that are simply too worn-out to be workable, garments that were too faddish and have long outlived their "in" year, perhaps even some items that no longer fit.

Your marginal pile is for items that may still have some life in them. The standard suggestion that you throw out anything you haven't worn in two years may not be valid. Perhaps you simply wore something to death the first season it was purchased and just got tired of it. If it's a quality item, let it rest for a while then bring it back into your active wardrobe, spruced up with new accessories. Perhaps you simply never found the right tie or blouse to go with a particular suit. In that case, resolve to take the time to look again and find the right accessory.

Maybe there is something in this pile that could benefit from alterations—a jacket with wide lapels or men's pants that are too wide at the bottom. Something else might simply need a new zipper, new buttons, or a trip to the cleaners.

Give yourself one week to have these repairs taken care of; most dry cleaners have someone they can recommend to do simple alterations. If you find yourself with an item that is perfectly satisfactory except that you don't like it—a mushroom-colored suit that merges you with the walls, a garment that you associate with an unpleasant experience—then give it away.

CHARTING YOUR COURSE

Look through pile number three, the things you wear regularly; take stock of what you have, and note it in the appropriate space on the wardrobe inventory pages at the back of this book (see pages 280–83). You will begin to get a clear picture of what you have as well as what you need. If you run out of space listing all your ties, then you probably don't need to invest money in new ones. But if you see that you have only three good shirts, you should add at least one more on your next shopping trip. If only one blouse goes with your burgundy suit, then begin looking for another one.

As you are filling out the chart, try to determine when it is that you feel at a loss, dissatisfied with the choices you have to wear. Is it during rainy weather? Perhaps you need a new raincoat. Is it when you are packing to go out of town and realize that you have lots of nice clothes, but nothing that goes with anything else? In that case, concentrate on pieces that will pull everything together.

How about those occasions when you have an important presentation to make? Do you feel at a loss then? If so, perhaps you need to purchase a simple dark-colored suit that will give you some clout when the situation demands it.

These are all individual considerations, but they are worth taking the time to think through so you can find the "holes" in your wardrobe. Before you carry unwanted garments off to your favorite charity, take a last look at that pile of clothing discards and determine where you are going wrong, what you are buying consistently but not wearing. Are there a lot of ties and blouses that don't work well with what you have? Do you have lots of shoes that you bought on sale but that actually have no place in your career wardrobe?

Most people find their discard pile is filled with inexpensive, rather poorly made items that were purchased on impulse but simply didn't hold up or didn't work well with the classic items in their wardrobes. Many women buy blouses this way. A lot of men get in a rut and find they continue to buy the same burgundy-patterned tie over and over because they don't really know what else to try. Some people find they have spent unwisely on seasonal things—a heavy flannel suit that gets worn three or four times a winter, or a seersucker suit that's only good for two months.

Try on all the clothes in pile number three—the clothes you wear regularly—and determine which fit and which don't. Try some different combinations—the light-blue shirt with a crisp white collar (rather than the white one) with your solid navy suit. Or try a navy background tie with the gray suit.

Women should "break up" their suits. How about the black skirt with the camel jacket, or the burgundy with the gray? Look at the scarves and blouses you have. Often these can pull together the total look. If you're not sure about wearing the emerald-green blouse with the navy suit, wear a scarf that incorporates both colors to finish off the outfit.

Generally the darker colors will be more serviceable when you are mixing and matching. Try your suit jackets over your dresses for new combinations. Try each tie with every jacket you own.

What this is leading to is a clear picture of your wardrobe, with all its strengths and weaknesses. After you have given it some thought, make a list of your next five major wardrobe purchases. Stick to this plan. As you buy one item, add another to your "List of Five." Once you have suits in the basic colors, then you can think in terms of subtly patterned suits—plaid, herringbone, or tweed.

Whenever possible, take a small sample of the garment material from the trouser bottoms or shortened sleeves. Or snip some threads so that you can attach them to the back of your inventory card. This will help when you are choosing accessories. Don't depend on your memory to tell you whether the grays or the blues are the same.

Take your inventory card, your "next five" list, and your resolve with you when you go shopping. If you find an attractive scarf or tie that would work with two or three different suits or a versatile belt, then buy it. But stay with your List of Five for the major purchases, so you don't end up with yet another suit in a color that you don't need.

Once you have thought all this through, you will find you can make better use of your shopping time, eliminating the aimless wandering and the trying on of items you know you aren't going to buy. You might even enjoy the whole process.

Use the following sample wardrobes only as guides. Leave some room to display your own personality, and adapt your business look to the special needs of your industry and individual schedule. Think in terms of classic styles and versatile, appropriate accessories.

SAMPLE MAN'S BASIC WARDROBE

- [ ] Solid-colored navy suit
- [ ] Solid-colored gray suit
- [ ] Pin-striped navy or gray suit
- [ ] Navy blazer*
- [ ] 1 pair khaki trousers*
- [ ] 1 pair gray trousers*
- [ ] 4 white shirts

- [ ] 2 light-blue shirts
- [ ] 1 blue pinstripe shirt
- [ ] 1 pair black slip-on shoes
      or
  1 pair modified wing tips

- [ ] 4 pair black over-the-calf socks
- [ ] 2 pair navy over-the-calf socks
- [ ] 4 burgundy ties
- [ ] 1 navy tie
- [ ] Good quality briefcase
- [ ] All-weather coat

NEXT FIVE PURCHASES

- [ ] Camel blazer*
- [ ] Tan suit
- [ ] Subtle herringbone suit
- [ ] Cordovan shoes

- [ ] Additional shirts:
  2 white
  1 light blue
  1 light blue with white collar

*Not recommended for very conservative industries.

SAMPLE WOMAN'S BASIC WARDROBE

- [ ] 1 black suit
- [ ] 1 tan suit
- [ ] 1 burgundy suit
- [ ] Red blouse
- [ ] Pink blouse
- [ ] Cream blouse
- [ ] Black-and-tan dress (two-piece if possible)

- [ ] Burgundy-and-tan dress (two-piece if possible)
- [ ] Black pumps or sling backs
- [ ] Burgundy pumps or sling backs
- [ ] 6 pair neutral-toned hose
- [ ] 3 silk scarves (with at least 2 colors in them)
- [ ] Good quality briefcase or purse
- [ ] All-weather coat

NEXT FIVE PURCHASES

- [ ] 1 unconstructed red jacket
- [ ] 1 gray suit
- [ ] Taupe-colored pumps
- [ ] 2 more silk scarves
- [ ] 1 deep-blue, green, or fuchsia blouse

SHOPPING

Sooner or later it will be time to stop planning and start shopping. Most of us, conditioned by fruitless excursions to stores and shopping malls, have come to dread the shopping trip. But I think you will find that having a plan and the determination to stick to it makes a real difference.

Before you select a store for your expedition, stop and think about what you already know about the shops in your area, either from advertisements, word of mouth, or your own past experience. Select three or four stores that are likely to have the kind of clothes you are looking for at prices you can afford. You'll do yourself a favor if you choose stores in the same shopping mall or at least in the same area of the city, so you won't waste valuable time in your car. As simple as it sounds, use the telephone to inquire about current stock. See if the stores have any of your targeted purchases in your size.

You might want to "scout out" some of your choices during a lunch hour, to give yourself an idea of what a particular store offers, the brands it carries, and the range of prices. By all means use the store's displays as a source of ideas for your own wardrobe. You don't have to buy the exact shirt or blouse a suit is displayed with; but you can certainly note updated accessories and colors.

SHOPPING ON THE ROAD

If you travel frequently, you will be tempted sooner or later to do some shopping away from home. You may find yourself with a nice block of uninterrupted time if a meeting is canceled or if you finish with a client earlier than you expected. The temptation may be especially strong if you come from a smaller city and find yourself in Dallas or New York with time on your hands and a credit card in your wallet.

Remember that the glamor of shopping in a distant city may be offset by the impossibility of making exchanges or returns if the garment falls apart after one cleaning, or by the difficulty of having alterations done, which normally may have been included in the price of the garment.

SHOPPING SERIOUSLY

For serious shopping, allow yourself at least two or three hours. Don't ever shop when you are depressed; that's like going grocery shopping when you are hungry. You'll end up indulging yourself with some expensive mistakes.

Dress in the kind of clothes you are going to be buying. If you are looking for a business dress, don't wear jeans and sandals. If you're after a three-piece suit, don't wear your Nikes and jogging suit. Women should remember to wear undergarments similar to those they normally wear with business clothes. You will also notice that the better dressed you are, the better you are treated by the salespeople.

Overall, you can expect to find the best selection of clothing in August and September, as stores put out their fall merchandise. This is when they have their largest inventories of seasonless or year-round styles and fabrics. The traditional retail sale months are January, early July, and November; at this time most retailers' selections are likely to be at their low point, too.

Always inquire early on about a store's return policy. Most reputable stores will allow you to return merchandise for full refund, and exchange for credit on your charge account as long as the garment is unworn and you have the sales slip. A good store will always take back any garment that does not survive laundering, dry cleaning, or reasonable wear, so long as you have followed the directions for care. The exceptions would be discount stores, which frequently have very restrictive return policies. Some permit only exchanges, and often those must be accomplished within a very short period of time. In general, department stores are much better about taking returned goods than boutiques, since their volume is much greater.

If you are not treated courteously in a store, speak to the department manager or store owner. It's nice to be equally outspoken about good service you receive. Quality stores appreciate customer feedback.

FOR MEN

The sales expertise in men's clothing stores is usually of a better quality than that in comparably priced women's shops, but don't count on it. Evaluate the available help carefully. Determine whether the salesman is going to be of any real help in making suggestions or will simply ring up a sale. If you find a helpful salesperson, cultivate him and become one of his regulars. But always have a clear idea of what you want, what looks good on you and what fits you well.

Begin by telling the salesman what you are looking for. The more positive you sound, the more likely you will get what you want. Don't hesitate to say no, even if you are being "double-teamed" by a pair of helpful, considerate salespeople. It is you, not they, who must wear and pay for the garment. The vast majority of men's clothes are still purchased by women. If you bring along an advisor, make sure that she or he is someone who understands your industry and your particular business environment and is someone with very good taste.

FITTING CHECKLIST

- ☐ Try on every garment you buy.
- ☐ Check the fit in a three-way mirror.
- ☐ Move around, sit down, stretch.
- ☐ See how the garment feels. There should be no pulls, no uncomfortable bunching up of material.
- ☐ Notice how the garment looks. There should be no bulges, no wrinkles.
- ☐ Do you like the garment, or are you simply relieved to find something that fits? If you are not enthused about adding it—whatever it is—to your wardrobe, don't buy it.

It is a good idea to get in the habit of saving all your sales slips to facilitate any returns you have to make. Follow care and cleaning instructions religiously. If the suit wears out within two years and if it has not been overly dry cleaned, you should return it to the store. It is unrealistic to think you will receive a full refund of your purchase price; but you should receive some credit toward another purchase. Most stores should recognize their own merchandise, particularly if the store's label is in the garment, but a sales slip will make things a lot easier.

The actual amount of credit or refund you receive will probably be negotiated. Your manner and whether you have been a good customer will play a part in the final determination.

FOR WOMEN

Once you get inside a store, with your updated inventory chart, you will have to do some on-the-spot evaluations of the sales expertise available. If you are lucky enough to have a favorite store, perhaps you have established a rapport with a knowledgeable saleswoman. If so, congratulations. Knowledgeable salesladies seem to be a dying breed, replaced too often by gum-chewing automatons whose main concern is keeping an eye on the clock.

Everyone has had the annoying experience of being "helped" by a well-intentioned but incompetent salesperson who thinks everything looks "great" and assures you that every flaw "is supposed to look that way." If the store is out of your skirt size, she assures you that they run large and you can buy the 8, not the 10. If the fit is less than perfect, she tells you that's the way "they" are wearing jackets this year or that it's a "European" cut.

Occasionally you will get lucky and find someone who really does help—who will swap the 8 for the 10, the black for the navy, or remember that a new shipment of blouses has not yet been unpacked. She might even offer a knowledgeable opinion about a garment in which you are interested. Sometimes you might hit the jackpot and find a sales fashion consultant who has a keen sense of style and knows what will work on you. She is worth cultivating, because she can save you a lot of money and time. This type of person is more likely to be found in better shops or small owner-operated boutiques.

If your saleswoman is offering advice, notice how she is dressed. If she is wearing ultra-fashionable attire, she probably has very little to tell you about professional dressing.

Finally, decide on your own how much "help" you want or need from whatever sales help is available. Department stores are usually more impersonal, with very little true "help." You can generally leave anonymously, because no one has come to your assistance. Specialty stores and boutiques generally have better-trained staffs, but there is also more pressure to purchase.

You may be better off shopping by yourself, but a trusted friend or an enlightened husband who knows your style and your business can be helpful. Remember, business shopping is better regarded as serious business than as a social occasion.

TO THE DRESSING ROOM

Before you make your selection, ask if the store has a posted "limit" on the number of items you may take into the dressing room. Occasionally, if you are in the store during a time when it is not especially busy, the sales staff will make an exception for you, especially if you look solid and respectable. Those limits are generally imposed to guard against shoplifters and young teenagers who like to cart half the sportswear department into the fitting room and while away a Saturday afternoon. If the store sticks to its guns, see if the salesperson will hold on to your other choices or if there is a rack you can reach without having to leave the dressing room area.

Some discount stores or outlets have instituted the communal dressing room, which sacrifices your privacy for their convenience in "policing" the changing areas. Some women find this mildly annoying; others find it very off-putting. If it really bothers you, then don't shop at stores that use this sort of arrangement. But you can take comfort knowing that no matter how many people are in the fitting room, you will always find people who look a whole lot better and a whole lot worse than you do.

The lighting in most store dressing rooms seems designed to make everyone, no matter what the hue of her skin, look like a freshly plucked chicken. A notable exception to this is Neiman-Marcus, which has installed soft, flattering lights in its dressing rooms, a move so simple and so smart it's surprising other stores haven't followed suit. But if your store is not so "enlightened," see if there is a mirror in better lighting where you can check the fit of the garment you are trying on. One of the few dicta in purchasing clothing is never to buy anything until you have viewed it in a three-way mirror. Always know how you are being viewed from the back and the sides because more people will see you from these angles than from the front.

CHECKLIST

☐ Does the garment fit you or is it simply the correct size? There is a difference.

☐ Is it versatile?

☐ Move around. Anything too tight will look cheap, regardless of how much you pay for it. Anything too large will look dowdy.

☐ Check out your problem areas. Does the garment flatter you there?

☐ Sit down. Your rib cage expands and can cause buttons to pull in front.

☐ Take a handful of the material in your hand and squeeze it. If the wrinkles remain, you are contemplating a purchase that will bring you misery.

☐ Does this garment fit into your wardrobe plan? Is it on your Next Five List?

☐ If you are doubtful, remove the garment and say no thanks. You are not obligated to buy anything.

Remember, you don't create a successful wardrobe by buying clothes you *like*, you do it by *investing* in clothing that you *love*.

CATALOG SHOPPING

Shopping from catalogs is gaining in popularity. Certainly it has its advantages, particularly if you live in an area where there is a limited selection of good clothing stores. Or, if you have worn a particular manufacturer's clothing before and know that a size 10 dress always fits or that a 16-34 shirt will be exactly right, then you can save yourself time and perhaps money.

But stick to the well-established names: J. C. Penney, Speigel, Neiman-Marcus, L. L. Bean or well-known regional department or specialty stores, like Rich's, Jordan-Marsh, and Macy's.

Mail-order shopping services have a very high mortality rate—and it is often true that the slicker the catalog, the slipperier those behind it. Make sure you know something about any company from which you intend to order. Use the toll-free numbers that are given and ask questions. Call or write to consumer protection agencies to report any fraud or misrepresentation.

If you want to check out a particular catalog outlet, start off by ordering a small, inexpensive item first. See how long it takes for your order to be filled and how the quality of the item compares with the "look" of the catalog. Remember, professional photography can cover a multitude of manufacturing sins. Good lighting and a size 8 fashion model can make anything look good. But what matters ultimately is how the garment fits you and what the fabric looks and feels like. You really can't determine these things until you see the garment for yourself.

If you are a borderline size, select the larger size, rather than the smaller one. Returns and exchanges may be a problem—in terms of the time involved. If your mail-order white linen suit doesn't reach you until September, it's not going to do you much good. But the good quality catalog merchants will have a generous return policy, some even paying the shipping on returned items; and often they will ship within ten days of receiving the order.

Generally, I advise you to approach catalog shopping with your eyes open. Take precautions: Stay with established companies, and save all your receipts and acknowledgments. If your shopping time or your access to good clothing stores is limited, then catalogs will be a blessing.

5

FABRIC:
IF IT LOOKS GOOD,
WEAR IT

Every business person needs a working knowledge of fabrics, to ensure top value in clothing. Certain fabrics are longer-lasting, more comfortable, or easier to care for than others, but each one has a list of pluses and minuses.

If you travel a great deal, then wrinkle-resistance will be important to you; if you're on a tight budget, then you want a fabric that will not need dry cleaning too frequently.

Fabrics are either *natural*, from animal or vegetable sources, or *man-made*, with a chemical base. But there is a third group of *fabric blends* that, properly manufactured, can combine the rich look and the comfort of the naturals with the easy-care properties of the man-mades.

The textile industry has made great strides in just the last few years in perfecting blends. When wool is blended with polyester the color and the texture of the wool overpower the polyester to give the cloth a rich look and feel; yet the polyester content prevents excessive wrinkling. Usually the best blends have a natural fiber content higher than that of the synthetic or man-made fiber—say fifty-five percent natural with forty-five percent man-made, although many fine suiting fabrics are fifty-five percent Dacron polyester and forty-five percent cotton or wool.

In our seminars, we pass around a group of fifteen different fabrics, both natural and man-made, and ask the participants to identify each one. They are allowed as much time as they need and are encouraged to handle all of the samples. The outcome of this "test" hardly ever varies. Most people are not able to identify even half of the fabrics correctly. Time and time again the participants confuse acrylic with wool, polyester with silk, and rayon with cotton. It's not that these people are unaware of the differences between natural and man-made fabrics; it is simply that good-quality man-made fibers and blends of man-made and natural fibers are so attractive they fool almost everyone.

FEAR OF POLYESTER

The very word "polyester" sends chills down the spines of most of us. The word itself has become synonymous with cheap or tasteless. When polyester double-knits first came on the scene in the late sixties, designers and manufacturers went overboard. Polyester's arrival in the marketplace coincided with the period when women were entering the labor force in huge numbers, and the easy-care, throw-it-on-the-floor, stomp-on-it then watch-it-bounce-back characteristics of polyester made it seem like the answer to everyone's prayer. No more ironing, no more wrinkles. Polyester double-knits were everywhere, on everyone. It was virtually impossible to find a garment made of one-hundred-percent natural fibers.

Gradually, though, both consumers and the textile industry began to notice that double-knit polyester jackets hung like cardboard boxes, with no real fit, no movement. Skirts and trousers were always uncomfortable. This fused fabric didn't breathe. It was hot and sticky in the summer and cold and clammy in the winter.

Slowly but surely, the textile industry began to make improvements in polyester and to move in the direction of blends—polyester mixed with silk, linen, cotton, wool, or even rayon—to provide durability, wrinkle-resistance, and comfort.

The most desirable fabrics for business clothes are those that look, feel and respond like natural fibers—whether they are or not is unimportant.

NATURAL FIBERS

Natural fibers have either vegetable sources, like cotton and linen, or animal sources, like silk and wool. Fabrics made from these fibers are woven. All four of these natural fibers have some common characteristics:

- They absorb moisture well but dry slowly.
- They are long-lasting.
- They will shrink if not properly laundered or cleaned.
- They require pressing or ironing.
- They soil easily.
- They mold themselves to the body attractively.
- They cannot be heat set, to make permanent pleats or tucks.

COTTON

Cotton is a strong, comfortable fabric that takes dye well and is quite absorbent. It is the most comfortable of all the natural fibers and quite versatile. Cotton has a nice mat finish, but it will wrinkle easily unless it is chemically treated, or Sanforized; and it is susceptible to mildew. It can be laundered or dry cleaned and is reasonably priced.

Cotton takes several different forms:

- *Broadcloth* and *oxford cloth*, commonly used for shirts and dresses.
- *Pincord* and *poplin*, heavier fabrics, often used for suits or jackets.
- *Seersucker*, used for suits, although it is far less desirable than pincord or poplin.

Cotton suits will generally show signs of wear after six months of use, so purchase them selectively. Pure cotton shirts or dresses should be purchased slightly larger than your actual size to correct for shrinkage.

An all-cotton shirt is very comfortable. If it is not starched, it will look wilted at the end of the day. All one-hundred-percent cotton shirts need some starch for a full day's wear, although heavy starch will shorten the life span considerably.

Cotton and polyester blends resist wrinkling and are fine for the man or woman who doesn't have a perspiration problem. However, they still need light starch and ironing for a professional appearance, especially on the collar, cuffs, and front placket. Giving them a shake after removing them from the dryer doesn't do the job.

WOOL

Wool is strong and resilient and is the longest-lasting natural fiber available. Since it can be processed into so many different weights and finishes, it is quite versatile. Wool breathes, takes dyes well and can provide a great deal of warmth. The harder finishes, like wool gabardine, are worn year-round. The softer finishes, like tweed, are worn only in cold weather.

Harder finishes are put through an additional process that twists the fibers and provides the smoother, "harder" look that gives a firmer feel to a garment. They are always an excellent choice for business because they are more formal than the softer finishes. Harder finishes give many years of use before they begin to show wear.

Harder finished fabrics:

- *Wool crepe* is a lighter fabric, used frequently in women's suits.
- *Worsted wools*, with a harder finish, are excellent choices for men's and women's suits.
- *Wool gabardine* is a diagonal twill weave done on wool that is very beautiful and very long-lasting in all suiting selections.

Softer finished fabrics:

- *Flannel* has a soft finish and is used in cold-weather suits.
- *Camel's hair* is used in jackets and topcoats.
- *Cashmere* is the most expensive and delicate wool fabric available, possessing a soft, luxurious feel; it is beautiful for jackets, coats and sweaters.
- *Mohair* and *angora* are not suited to conservative office wear.

Wool is susceptible to moth damage and must be carefully stored in moth-proof bags or chests. Because of shrinkage, wool should be dry cleaned but only about three times a year. Between cleanings, it should be aired out and, when necessary, professionally pressed, so actually the maintenance need not be terribly expensive.

Wool blends are very popular choices for suits and dresses; but if you are purchasing a topcoat, you are well advised to stay with one-hundred-percent wool, since this will provide the maximum warmth.

SILK

Silk is a strong, luxurious, and very expensive natural fiber, with a characteristically rich look and texture. It has a natural luster that is difficult to duplicate, but it lacks the durability of cotton or wool. It takes color very well, although it is not colorfast, and it can be processed into many different weights and finishes.

Silk wrinkles very easily and usually needs cleaning after each wearing. The fibers are easily weakened by perspiration. White and light-colored silk blouses may be carefully hand-laundered, but darker colors must be dry cleaned; otherwise, the water will bleed the color out of the silk.

Silk is commonly used in women's dresses, blouses, and scarves, and in men's ties and handkerchiefs. Scarves require one-hundred-percent silk, as do men's ties, because the man-made fibers simply don't knot as well. Silk can be blended into jackets and suits and will lend a luxurious appearance to any other fabric with which it is combined—even if it is only five percent or ten percent of the fiber content. An all-silk suit, however, is usually impractical for business wear because it loses its shape and lacks durability.

Silk takes several forms:

- *Crepe de chine*—a very thin, luxurious material used for blouses and dresses.
- *Foulard*—generally associated with small geometric prints, often made into ties and scarves.

■ *Pure silk*—the most desirable because it is untreated and its appearance is unaltered. This is used for ties, dresses, blouses, and scarves and is often blended into jackets.

■ *Raw silk* is much thicker and has a duller finish that makes it a good choice in blends for dresses and women's and men's jackets.

Silk can "lift" any other fabric with which it is worn. The variation in silk prices often depends on whether the silk came from cultured or uncultured silkworms, something that relates to the silkworms' diets, rather than to their exposure to good music and art. The cultured worm has the costlier and more controlled diet and provides the more expensive, finer-textured silk. The uncultured worm is left to scrounge for food, and produces uneven thread. This plays a part in determining whether a silk item will cost twenty dollars or one hundred dollars.

LINEN

Linen is a strong, durable fabric, suitable only for warm-weather wear. Because it wrinkles extremely easily, linen requires some man-made fiber, like viscose or polyester, to be blended in with it, or it is virtually useless for office wear. Fashion books tell their readers that wrinkling is part of the beauty of linen, and even instruct women on how to wrinkle their linen garments. For casual wear, wrinkled linen is an individual's prerogative. For office wear, it won't work.

But when linen is properly blended it will look cool and crisp and remain relatively wrinkle-free. It generally gives a more casual look, and can be quite expensive. Linen blends are suitable for women's suits, blouses, and dresses and for men's blazers.

MAN-MADE FABRICS

Most textile manufacturers cringe at the word *synthetic*, preferring, instead, *man-made*, which does not have the unfortunate lime-green pantsuit associations of synthetic. Because of the advances in the textile industry, the better man-made fabrics bear little resemblance to the parade of horrors that gave polyester such a bad name a decade or so ago. The price of the man-made fabrics varies considerably; some of the best-looking ones approach the cost of natural fibers.

Man-made fabrics have chemical origins and are fused rather than woven. They are made to imitate the look of natural fibers with considerably less maintenance required. They share these characteristics:

- They blend well with natural fibers.
- They do not shrink.
- They require little or no ironing.
- They dry quickly and do not absorb moisture; thus they do not breathe, or allow air to circulate. This means they can be uncomfortable: cold in winter and hot in summer.
- They collect static electricity.
- They can be heat set, so pleats can be put in permanently.
- They may retain perspiration odors.

POLYESTER

This fabric takes more than twenty-five different forms and can be made to resemble silk, cotton, or linen. It blends well with all natural fibers, and is most valued for the fact that it does not wrinkle or shrink. Poorly made, it has a very unattractive chemical sheen; properly manufactured, it can have a rich-looking luster. When that occurs, it is a good choice for dresses and blouses and, when blended into wool, for suits and jackets. It is at its most unattractive when made into knits or fabrics with a shiny appearance.

Occasionally, when blended with cotton or wool, polyester will "pill" or actually separate from the natural fiber, especially around areas of stress or friction, like the neckline. Polyester is impervious to mildew or moth damage; but it can be uncomfortable, since it does not allow natural air circulation.

RAYON

This was the first of the man-made fibers. Because it lacks the chemical base the other man-mades have, it does allow for breathing and will look like a natural fabric. Rayon can appear like silk or cotton and is a good addition to a blend. Used by itself it will wrinkle; combined with polyester, viscose or nylon, it will hold its shape nicely. Rayon should always be dry cleaned so it won't shrink, sag, or lose its color. Once it has been laundered at home, it will never look the same. It is more commonly used in women's clothes than men's.

ACRYLIC

This man-made fiber very closely resembles wool when it is carefully manufactured. It is soft, warm, and easy to care for, and is a very good choice for people who are allergic to wool. Some forms of acrylic can be washed, but dry cleaning is recommended to help keep its shape. It can be made into sweaters or used the same way as wool—for suits, dresses, and coats.

LEATHER, SUEDE, AND ULTRASUEDE

Leather and suede come, of course, from animal skin; ultrasuede is a luxurious man-made fabric. For different reasons, none of the three is a good choice for business clothing, although leather is quite desirable for accessories—shoes, attaché cases, belts, and purses. However, leather jackets, vests, and skirts are much too casual and have too many negative associations to be effective business garb.

Suede, on the other hand, is too "Western" looking for business clothes and it soils easily. Suede shoes are too casual in men's styles and often too dressy in women's styles. Suede note pads are a good choice for business, but a suede briefcase is not.

Ultrasuede, which has the advantage of not needing professional dry cleaning, simply appears too country-club-like, whether it is worn by men or women. It is not the best business choice, even though it resists wrinkling and travels extremely well. Because ultrasuede is a fused chemical fabric, a cigarette burn will melt it, and the damage will be irreparable, which is not the case with a natural or blended fabric, which can be rewoven.

CORDUROY, VELVET, VELOUR, DENIM, SATIN, AND CHIFFON

These materials can be made from a number of different fibers or combinations of natural and man-made fibers; each has a characteristic texture.

Corduroy, generally, is too casual for office wear; it wears out and loses its shape quite rapidly. Velvet is too dressy for a professional look—it is better saved for evening wear. Velvet blazers have been popular for several years, but they are not a good office choice.

Other fabrics, like velour and denim, are best saved for leisure wear; satins and chiffons, even in scarves, are for evening wear only.

□ 6 □

COLOR: THE GOOD, THE BAD, AND THE NOT SO GOOD

Color is at once the most powerful component of a wardrobe and the most confusing. Choice of color is the major reason someone looks professional or not professional, appropriate or inappropriate. Confusion over color is the main reason we often find ourselves with closets full of things we never wear. Fabric is relatively easy to get a handle on, but color is more difficult.

Actually, color works hand in hand with fabric. The richest-looking color can be cheapened by a poor-quality material. The same ruby red that is soft and luxurious in a pure silk or silk lookalike appears tawdry and harsh in a shiny polyester. There is virtually no such thing as an ugly color; but there are colors that are inappropriate for a particular fabric, a particular business, or a particular individual.

The color question has been addressed in the last few years by the emergence of the "color-experts." It would certainly be simpler if these color analysts provided us with the final answers to color questions as they relate to business wear. But according to the color theories, authority colors like navy, black, and dark gray can be worn only by about twenty-five percent of the population. Where does that leave the other seventy-five percent, who need, on occasion, some powerful colors?

71

You can have a little fun with the four seasons concept (which categorizes people according to the seasons of the year) or any other color concept that someone develops. But it is a mistake to take it too seriously for business. It's also a costly error to spend a lot of money replacing cosmetics and a wardrobe because you are "out of season."

Anyone, actually, can wear any color. It is the value—the lightness or darkness, the intensity—of colors that must be varied.

In selecting colors for your business wardrobe stay with the basic colors as outlined in this chapter and accent with contrasting colors. You will also find that the colors that you like—the ones that make you feel good, the ones that people compliment you on—are your best colors. You simply need to learn how and when and where to wear them. Chances are, if you have a favorite tie or dress that looks terrific, and always brings compliments—it is probably because the color is right on you.

COLOR AND EMOTIONS

Our response to color is as much emotional as physical. Certain colors deliver messages in and of themselves that have absolutely nothing to do with the hair or skin tones of the individual wearing them. Darker colors generally convey more authority. Think of clerical black or the navy blue of police uniforms. Medium-range colors like blue or tan make us look friendly, more approachable. Large expanses of pastels make us look less serious, sometimes unprofessional, and are more suited for off-the-job looks.

Sometimes the emotional responses generated by a particular color or color combination are intensely personal and defy any attempt to explain them logically. One woman shudders at any dark green and tan color combination, because those were the colors of the parochial school uniforms she wore as a child. A man dislikes mint green because it was the color of the walls of the hospital room where he was once confined.

The business of color selection is not an exact science by any means, but it is possible to make some observations and come up with generalizations about colors and their use that have proven to be accurate.

BASIC WARDROBE COLORS

In selecting a business wardrobe use darker, more authoritative colors for the larger pieces—skirts, suits, and jackets. Save the brighter colors for accent—blouses, ties, pocket handkerchiefs. This will maximize the use you will get from each of your garments.

A woman's black suit worn on Monday with a rose-colored silk blouse and on Friday with a brilliant blue shirt will always look like two distinct outfits. A bright yellow suit will always look like a bright yellow suit, regardless of the blouse you wear with it. Similarly, a man can wear the same bright burgundy patterned tie with his navy suit on Tuesday and his gray suit on Thursday, and it will very likely look like two different ties.

BEST BASIC COLORS FOR WOMEN: SUITS, BLAZERS, AND SKIRTS

black	blue	beige and camel
burgundy	brown	gray

BEST BASIC COLORS FOR MEN: SUITS, JACKETS, AND TROUSERS

medium blue	beige and camel
navy	gray

These are not the only choices, but they should be regarded as the basics. There is no color that is totally off limits to women in business, but there are some colors that work better in smaller amounts as accent colors. An emerald green, for instance, may be great in a blouse but too strong in a suit. A pale-pink jacket looks too fragile for office wear, but the same color in a softly tied blouse would do wonders for a gray suit and a sallow complexion.

Men are more restricted in their color choices. Some colors, like green, detract from a business look. Solid brown is dangerous; it might work on an older man when used in a rich-looking fabric in just the right warm hue, but usually it has either a lower-class or country-squire look. The President of the United States can wear this color well, but he has age and the trappings of his office, as well as a very fine tailor to make it work.

Even though they seem to come "in" periodically, shirts in lavender, light green, and tangerine colors are not good business choices. Generally, for men, it's best to stick to the more traditional colors.

A key point to remember is that a business look does not have to be boring or clonelike. You don't have to wear only a white blouse or a white shirt with a dark gray pin-striped suit. A woman can wear a light gray, red, or purple blouse, appropriately accessorized. A man can choose a very light gray shirt, a pale blue shirt, or a white shirt with blue or red pinstripes. You can use accent colors so your outfits will still have the overall effect of authority, but won't be too drab and uninteresting.

The idea is to give yourself as many options as possible, so you can cultivate a professional look that is uniquely yours. Here's a good look at the basic colors and some good accent colors, along with some suggested do's and don'ts on incorporating them into your wardrobe.

BLACK

Black is the ultimate power color; yet only women can effectively wear it in the daytime. For men, it is simply too overpowering in anything but formal wear.

WOMEN

- *Do* use it for suits, skirts, blazers.
- *Do* accent with a bright color; this way black works well on all women.
- *Do* wear with a variety of bright colors and patterns.

MEN

- *Do not* buy for suits.
- *Do* select for leather accessories—belts, shoes, wallet, possibly briefcase.

WOMEN

■ *Do* wear year-round; it's a good color that requires a minimum of dry cleaning.

■ *Do* purchase it for leather accessories—shoes, purse, possibly briefcase.

■ *Do not* wear as accessories with navy suit or dress.

■ *Do not* wear next to the face.

BROWN

Brown is a good basic color that works better for women than for men. However, it requires an excellent fabric in order to look rich.

WOMEN

■ *Do* use for suits, skirts, blazers.

■ *Do* select a dark brown if hair is dark and coloring is dramatic.

■ *Do* select a lighter brown if hair is light and coloring more sallow.

■ *Do* always accent with bright colors.

■ *Do* use in tweeds and herringbones for a richer look.

MEN

■ *Do* use carefully and as a secondary color for suits.

■ *Do* use in tweeds and herringbones, as opposed to solids, for a richer look.

■ *Do* choose as background color in foulard ties when pairing them with tan or camel suits.

■ *Do* choose for accessories— belts, shoes, and especially briefcase.

BLUE

Blue is probably the universal favorite color, worn well by men and women. Literally everyone looks good in blue. For this reason, it is a frequent color choice for uniforms. Navy blue is a true power color, although it is stronger on men than women. Medium-tone blue becomes friendlier—a good choice on days you want to appear more approachable.

<table>
<tr><th>WOMEN</th><th>MEN</th></tr>
</table>

WOMEN

- *Do* select for suits, skirts, blazers, and dresses.
- *Do* reserve navy pinstripe for only your most powerful look.
- *Do* accent with bright or contrasting color.
- *Do* use for shoes or purse. Navy accessories can be worn with most colors, except black.
- *Do not* use for briefcase.

MEN

- *Do* choose for suits, trousers, and blazers.
- *Do* wear navy pinstripe as your most powerful look. Medium blue is friendlier.
- *Do* wear navy with a white shirt for another strong look.
- *Do* accent with light blue shirt rather than a white one when you want to appear friendlier and less formal.
- *Do* choose medium blue and navy as background colors in ties.
- *Do not* use for accessories.

BURGUNDY

Burgundy is one of the most flattering of the authoritative colors. When teamed with gray, it is one of the most elegant combinations for business.

WOMEN

- *Do* select for suits, skirts, blazers, dresses, and blouses.
- *Do* accent with bright or contrasting color.
- *Do* purchase for accessories— shoes, purse, briefcase. Burgundy can be worn with nearly every color.

MEN

- *Do* choose in ties, both as a background color and incorporated into a pattern. Burgundy ties will offer the richest look with gray, navy, and tan suits.
- *Do* use for belts, wallets, and briefcase in very deep burgundy.
- *Do not* use for suits, trousers, or blazers.
- *Do not* select for shoes.

BEIGES, TANS, AND CAMELS

This color group is one of the most versatile for men and women and works in larger pieces, like suits, shirts, blouses, and dresses. Some shades have brown undertones, others have yellow, pink, or green. Select the undertone that is most flattering to your skin.

WOMEN

- *Do* choose for suits, skirts, blazers, dresses, and blouses.
- *Do* use to appear businesslike without being overpowering.
- *Do* accent with bright colors, like red, fuchsia, or royal blue.
- *Do* choose in shoes and purse, especially in taupe.
- *Do not* select for briefcase.

MEN

- *Do* select for suits, trousers, and blazers.
- *Do* use as your friendliest basic color.
- *Do* use with a light-blue shirt (it's the best shirt color with this group).
- *Do* accent with burgundy or blue tie.
- *Do not* select for shoes, wallet, or briefcase.

GRAY

Gray is an excellent color for men or women to choose for major pieces. In darker charcoal shades it is a power color. Lightened up, it becomes more relaxed. It is a good choice for financial people or salespeople, because it conveys strength and stability.

WOMEN

- *Do* purchase for suits, skirts, blazers, dresses, and blouses.
- *Do* use as an authority color equivalent to navy.
- *Do* use with pinstripes—with care; it could become an overpowering look.

MEN

- *Do* buy for suits, trousers, and blazers.
- *Do* use with pinstripe for extremely powerful look.
- *Do* adopt as secondary background color in ties. Gray is excellent when incorporated into a pattern.

WOMEN	MEN
■ *Do* use for dresses and blouses, particularly if it's incorporated into a pattern.	■ *Do not* use for belts, shoes, or briefcase.
■ *Do* buy as secondary color for shoes and purse.	
■ *Do not* use for briefcase.	

CONTRASTING AND ACCENT COLORS

RED

Red is an excellent color for women, virtually a basic. But it is pretty much off limits to men, except as a toned-down background color in a patterned tie.

On women, red adds a real vibrancy and sparkle and is an excellent choice for dresses, blouses, and unconstructed jackets, since it pairs very well with black, navy, gray, and most shades of beige. It is not a good choice for shoes or purse because it becomes too striking. This same advice is true for a two-piece red suit. The suit will arrive before you do. However, a red jacket is a very versatile garment.

PINKS, ROSES

Deep, vibrant shades of pink and lighter shades of rose are good dress and blouse choices for women. They are also good as accent colors in scarves. But pink does not work for men, except possibly in shirts (and then only in a more fashionable or creative industry), or as a small pattern on a tie. Pinks and roses are not a good choice either for shoes, bags, or attaché cases.

GREEN

Green should not be worn by men in suits, shirts, jackets, or trousers in business situations. A small amount of green in a patterned tie may work, depending on the other colors.

Very dark bottle greens may be acceptable for women as secondary choices for a jacket or a dress. Bright green is more effective in smaller doses but often comes off as looking "preppy." Pastel greens often cause problems; they usually appear cheap except in the most beautiful of fabrics. This is because pastel green has so long been associated with spongy polyester pantsuits.

Many shades of green, like olive and greenish khaki, are rarely flattering next to anyone's face. They seem to drain all color from the skin. *Khaki*, in fact, is a Hindu word meaning "dusty," which is how most of us look when we wear it close to our faces. When khaki is in the tan family, rather than the green, it can successfully be worn with bright accents.

YELLOW

Yellow is an easy color to go wrong with, perhaps because there are so many variations. It should always be teamed with a basic color, like navy or gray, for business. It is also very important that you select the right value to flatter your skin shade.

Men should stay away from yellow for business wear, except as a background color for a tie. Women should avoid yellow for suits, but may use it with other colors, selectively in dresses and blouses. It is never a good choice for leather accessories—shoes, purses, attaché cases—since it looks too informal.

PEACH, APRICOT, ORANGES

The soft orangey shades should be avoided by men except in very small amounts on a tie or in a pocket handkerchief. Women can use the colors selectively in blouses and dresses, to work with navy, gray, brown, and occasionally black. Very young women should avoid a soft peach color, since it can lend a fragile air; it is not a good choice for leather accessories. True orange is good only in sportswear.

PURPLES, MAUVES

Very deep purples work best in small amounts—for men, they should be limited to accents in tie patterns, never in shirts or suits. Although purple has become a fashion color in recent years, it has not quite worked its way into the mainstream and needs to be approached with caution.

In a mauve, it is a good secondary choice for women's suits, dresses or blouses. Pastel shades like lilac and lavender are best held to a minimum except when combined with other colors in a patterned blouse. Solid lavender, in particular, has sexual and political connotations that make it a bad choice for men and not a particularly recommended one for women.

WHITE AND OFF-WHITE

White is a traditional summer color in suits and jackets for women, although a winter white is correct year-round. Yet white does require a great deal of dry cleaning, so it is probably better used in shirts for men or blouses for women. Women can wear white suits in the daytime, but for men, white suits should be worn only after 6:00 P.M. in the summer.

White is actually too stark for most women to wear, unrelieved, close to their faces, unless they are tanned, black or have naturally dark complexions. An interesting piece of jewelry at the neck can liven up the color. The best advice for women is to select a shade that is slightly darker than the color of their teeth, which may mean an ecru. It will prove much more flattering. A scarf at the neck will also soften the effect of white.

White is never appropriate for shoes for either men or women, except for leisure wear. Even with a white business suit, shoes should be navy or black. It is particularly unacceptable for business in a sandal, nor should it be used for belts or purses.

PATTERNS

Whether you opt for stripes, plaids, or patterns, the guiding precept is subtlety. Men and women may use small, subtle plaids for suits. The plaid should be regular in design, and the garment should be made so that the plaids match exactly at the seams. **Glen plaid** is the best. A man's plaid suit should never be purchased with the idea of wearing the suit jacket with another pair of trousers, since the combination will never look right. Men should also avoid plaids on shirts and ties. Women may wear plaids very selectively in blouses, skirts, and scarves, but the look is definitely more casual.

Herringbone is a very subtle, classic pattern that is both elegant and sophisticated. In heavier fabrics, it is a very good purchase for both men and women in blazers. In lighter weights, herringbone is an enduring suit pattern, especially if the pattern is very subtle. Muted grays are the richest-looking. Tweeds are also a very rich pattern usually found in blazers rather than suits.

Stripes can work very well to set off dark suits. Men may use very thin pinstripes in suits to enhance the authority of a navy or a gray suit. In fact, this is the ultimate power look. Former Secretary of State Alexander Haig, by anyone's reckoning a man who understood power and its trappings, was very partial to pin-striped suits. A white **pinstripe** is the most powerful; a multicolored pinstripe is friendlier.

Women can wear stripes in blouses and dresses very well. They give a clean, crisp look. Nevertheless, I would recommend buying only one or two pinstripe suits at most. The look can become an overpowering one when worn too frequently. Stripes should always be narrow and generally vertical.

Prints are best used as small dots and **foulards**—the classic geometric Ivy League look. For women, small abstract prints are a very sophisticated look. A classic print should never be larger than the head of a pencil eraser, except in an abstract shape for women (the ink blot, for instance). Women may wear prints in a blouse or dress, men can choose them in a tie.

□ 7 □

CAMOUFLAGING FIGURE PROBLEMS

There are very few "perfect" bodies—male or female—walking the corporate hallways or, for that matter, decorating the silver screen. In fact, the perfect female body of today—tall, firm, and muscular—was not a desirable body twenty years ago. Just as there are trends in clothing, there are also trends in body sizes and shapes.

Sometimes the "look" for women is that of the petite, busty cheerleader. Other times it's that of the long-legged bean pole. Men haven't experienced quite the same body trends as women, but they have had their share of media pressure to conform to a standard "ideal."

No wonder all of us have agonized about our bodies. Few have ever been able to measure up to the ideal. We can't alter our basic body proportions—arm and leg length and general bone structure. But we can, through the use of camouflage techniques in dressing, proportion our bodies so that they are attractive. It is simply a matter of mastering the art of emphasizing good features and playing down the weaker ones. Proportion and camouflage have to do with the eye, not the measuring tape or scale.

Proportion dressing for both men and women means a balance of color, style, and fabric that keeps the eye skimming over the figure problems and stopping at the best parts of the physique. Obviously, no one item of clothing can make a sylph out of someone who is one hundred pounds overweight. But care in selecting style, fabric, and color and attention to some key details can make the difference between a polished, sophisticated look and one that is unattractive and slovenly.

Our company once consulted with an executive who weighed three hundred pounds and who was very frank in saying he was *not* planning to lose weight. He had tried to diet time and time again but it was too discouraging and actually interfered with his work. He had decided the better plan was to work with what he had—all three hundred pounds of it.

We advised him that he would have to spend more time and money to clothe himself professionally than many of our clients. Nevertheless it could be done.

And it was—quite effectively. First of all, we cautioned him to be scrupulous in avoiding sloppiness. We gave him the mental picture of the actor Sebastian Cabot and told him to visualize himself in much the same way—extremely dignified, fastidious, refined.

We took him to tall and large men's specialty shops so he could be assured of suits that were properly fitted. We also suggested that he have his shirts custom-made, so the shirttails would be long enough to accommodate his size, and the buttons wouldn't pull across his stomach. We steered him toward extremely well-fitting suits in navy and charcoal gray, both solids and very thin pinstripes. Too wide a stripe would have made him look like a circus clown, but the very thin stripes gave the desired look of dignified solidity. It was crucial that the suits not fit tightly. Because he had a protruding stomach, we told him to stay away from off-the-rack vests, since they would never fit properly. However, when he was ready for custom-made suits, a well-fitted vest could be very slimming.

We also advised him never to wear his trousers lower than his navel. Some men try to fool themselves into believing they still wear a 36 waist by moving the waistband underneath their stomach. Doing this simply accentuates the stomach and looks very sloppy.

To ensure his neat, carefully finished look, our overweight client had to avoid wrinkles, so we helped him select good quality blends—fifty-five percent Dacron and forty-five percent wool—for his suits. This combination contained sufficient wool to give the fabric a natural look, one that would attractively mold to his body, but also enough man-made fiber to keep it wrinkle-free.

We recommended only very crisp white shirts or very light blue ones, both with foulard ties. His shirts had to be one-hundred-percent cotton so the cuffs and collar could be starched well. Substantial dark lace-up shoes completed the total look; a thin-soled, slip-on style would have looked too fragile on such a large man.

The end product was a man with an appealing quality of substance who was well-proportioned. He still weighed three hundred pounds, but he looked dignified rather than comical.

If the right clothing can make someone a hundred pounds overweight look good, imagine how much simpler it is to camouflage an extra twenty pounds, a skinny neck, large hips, or a short waist. These are all common problems that can be minimized, often normalized, by proportion dressing.

Fortunately for the professional with something to hide, it is the classic styles that work best on practically any body type. The time-proven classical cuts are most flattering to all figure types. When these styles are used with natural fibers and good quality blends, coupled with appropriate colors and patterns, the effect is stunning. The garments will skim over the body. If you are trying to camouflage a figure fault, you are well advised to buy the very best quality you can afford in the garment that covers that particular area. The better quality and attention to fine details your extra dollars will buy is a good investment.

PROPORTION DRESSING FOR MEN

The clothes that men have to select from are nearly always more flattering to varied body types than those available to women. But even within the range of good, classic styling, there are some guidelines that should be followed to make you look your best.

HEAVY MEN

- Stay with dark and medium colors for suits; leave the light tans and the pale grays to the slimmer men. Pinstripes are fine, as long as they are very thin.

- Never wear your clothes too tight; this will simply emphasize your extra weight. If you have a hard time finding clothes that fit, try a store that specializes in large and tall sizes.

- Suits are more slimming than strongly contrasting blazers and trousers, which tend to cut you in half and draw attention to your midsection. When you want to wear a blazer, select a navy one to wear with medium gray trousers.

- Wear a classic two-button jacket rather than the more European-influenced three-button style. The two-button jacket shows more shirt and gives a better proportion; the three-button is boxy-looking and cut for slim bodies.

- Choose jackets and blazers with a natural shoulder look—only slightly padded. Stay away from double-breasted jackets; this style adds weight, since it means an extra seven layers of fabric across the front.

- Stay with inside flap pockets on the hips. Outside patch pockets will attract the eye to the hips, often a problem area for heavier men.

- Be careful with vests. Properly fitted, they can be slimming on men whose weight is not concentrated in a bulge over their waistline. But if that's where you carry your weight, the vest will only accentuate your problem. If you do choose a vest, make certain that it overlaps the waistband on your trousers and that your shirt never shows between the vest and trousers. Buttons should not pull or gap.

- Select straight pockets, rather than slanted ones, on your trousers.

Anything that is skimpy or too small will make a large person appear larger. This man's tie is too short and his button-down shirt is a little too tight around the collar. His jacket is too small and his waistband should not be below the navel.

There's a genuine elegance to a large man when he dresses well. This shirt is properly fitted and diminishes his middle section. His shoulders appear broader. A striped tie, white shirt and well-polished shoes are important accessories. Without his mustache he has a more executive appearance.

- Avoid side vents on jackets. The single center vent, a hallmark of classic jackets, is much more flattering. Side vents make you look wider.

- Avoid cuffs on your trousers, unless you have sufficient height to balance your weight. Cuffs make men look shorter and often heavier.

- Be particularly careful that your shirt collars are large enough so you don't look as though you have been stuffed into your shirt. A tight collar will emphasize heavy jowls. Try a half size or full size larger. If you have difficulty getting shirts to fit, consider having them custom-made.

- If you are short and heavy, don't wear a full beard even if you are in an industry that will tolerate one.

- Suspenders give a very classy look on suits and will allow you to gain and lose weight more easily. They will replace your belt. Most good quality suspenders come with one set of buttons to sew on to your trousers, and your tailor can sew buttons on to the rest of your suits. However, don't consider skipping the buttons for clip-on suspenders. They are the equivalent of clip-on ties.

Don't worry about your extra pounds. Instead, concentrate on your carriage and pay attention to your garments. Henry VIII believed that only men who were substantial in girth could ever be substantial in life.

SHORT MEN

There are too many successful short men in business for lack of height to be used as an excuse to fail. A well-groomed short man with energy and direction has every reason to succeed.

Men who are short and slight should avoid the appearance of callowness, extreme youth, or fragility. Short men with a stockier build want to make sure that they don't look rotund. One short man we consulted with found he did better when he shopped in the boys' department rather than in the men's. The clothing was better-proportioned for his size and required fewer alterations. It cost less, too. Gradually, as his earnings improved, our client began to have his clothing made to measure. This allowed him a better choice of fabric—something harder to find in boys' departments. He also found it worth his while to spend more on very nice accessories—attaché case, shoes, and silver pen—since these things enhanced his stature.

Short men can look every bit as professional as their taller counterparts, if they pay attention to these details:

- Hard or smooth finish fabrics, like worsted wools, in darker colors, are better choices than light-colored "fuzzy" or tweed jackets and suits. Keep the attention around the face, with crisp clean collars and fine silk ties.

- Shirt collars should be in proportion to your size. Don't wear them too long or with a collar spread that is too wide. Ties should not reach below your waistband.

- Solid-color suits will give the illusion of length more effectively than a jacket and contrasting trousers. Plaids should be avoided.

- Avoid double-breasted suits: They will simply add bulk around the middle that only a taller man can tolerate.

- Natural shoulders, with slight padding, are best for jackets; exaggerated shoulder pads look ridiculous.

- Be very careful that trousers and sleeves are the proper length. If they are worn too long, they will give you a waiflike air.

- Wear only uncuffed pants; cuffs tend to "shorten" the man wearing them.

- Accessories must be in proportion. Avoid carrying an oversized briefcase.

Shorter men should approach double-breasted jackets and suits with caution. This styling broadens the midsection. His briefcase is a little too wide for his size. The paisley tie is too broad and the pattern is not muted enough.

A two-piece pinstripe suit in a darker color is extremely effective, both visually and professionally. This man's briefcase is scaled to his size and the foulard tie is rich-looking and very appropriate. His shirt collar and cuffs are crisp and well-starched.

TALL MEN

Height can be an advantage, but good carriage is the key. A tall, thin man must avoid looking gawky or ill-at-ease with his size. A tall, heavy man must never look sloppy or self-conscious.

Special attention should be accorded to length—of shirt sleeves, jacket sleeves, trousers, ties, and vests. Each must be correctly fitted. A suit jacket or blazer should cover the buttocks. Make sure that socks don't display long, hairy legs.

A tall man needs to pay extra attention to trouser length. This man's trousers are too short and his shoes are too casual for business. His pocket scarf is cavalier; there's too much showing and the pattern is loud. He also needs a haircut.

A well-fitted suit proportions all figure types. This man now looks in control of his appearance. His striped tie adds interest to his solid suit and the pocket handkerchief is discreet and correct.

- A tall man can wear both hard and soft finished fabrics equally well, and he can take his pick from among all the basic business colors.

- If a less formal look is appropriate, a tall man can wear a blazer and contrasting trousers very effectively.

- Subtle glen plaids can be very becoming on a tall man. If he is extremely thin, he ought to avoid narrow pinstripes except in shirts.

- A double-breasted jacket is very becoming to a tall, thin man.

- Accessories must always be in proportion. A large man needs a large briefcase: One that is too small will look like a toy.

PROPORTION DRESSING FOR WOMEN

The adoption of classic styles by professional women gives them the advantages of good cut and fit and the minimal fashion changes that men have enjoyed for years. The fact that women have a wider range of colors and accessories from which they can choose gives them lots of flattering options.

It helps for a woman to think of her body in thirds: neck to waist, waist to hem, and hem to shoe. The most balanced look occurs when each of these parts is in proportion with the others.

UNDERNEATH IT ALL

Proper undergarments are essential for a good smooth fit—no matter what your size. Panties should fit loosely enough so that the elastic never cuts into your waist or legs. If it does, the line of your panties is likely to be visible beneath your skirt or dress. Lace and trim should be discreet, never bulky.

Regardless of your bust size, a properly fitted bra is crucial to the fit of your clothes. It should give you firm, comfortable support, but the straps should not dig into your shoulder or back. You need a smooth line under blouses and dresses. Make sure the material of your bra is thick enough so that your nipples don't show through the fabric.

Tailored half slips are the best choice. Lace should be smooth, so your dress will lie flat. Nothing can ruin the look of an outfit faster than a slip that shows—no matter how pretty it is. Try on your slip with your shortest dress; if it shows, hem it from the top by cutting off the elastic and restitching. Half slips are more comfortable than full slips, and there are, of course, no straps to fall. But you should have a plain camisole to wear with sheer blouses or dresses.

I recommend buying all undergarments in beige or flesh tone only. This neutral color maintains a fresh look longer and will never be obvious underneath your clothing. White tends to look dingy after only a few washings. Vividly colored undergarments are very limiting.

Girdles are outdated curiosities, and they belong to a bygone era. Good riddance! They were uncomfortable and didn't really make a woman look thinner; they simply pushed her flesh around in unnatural positions. They also gave a hard and unnaturally immobile appearance to a woman's body. If your clothes are properly fitted, you won't ever need a girdle. If you want to make your tummy firmer, buy control-top panty hose or start exercising.

PROBLEM AREAS

Many women are the correct weight for their height, but simply have figure problems.

Large Busts—The sex goddess look is at odds with a professional business look. If you have a large bust, don't accentuate it by wearing tight sweaters, V-necked shirts or ruffled blouses. Instead, buy blouses and dresses of soft, nonclingy material, and wear them with jackets or blazers.

Thin Neck—Look for blouses and dresses with interesting necklines or collars: a tie bow collar, a high-necked cowl, a mandarin collar, even a discreet bit of lace will be attractive. Avoid V-necks and collarless blouses.

Thick Ankles or Heavy Legs—Avoid shoes with an ankle strap or an instep strap; plain pumps will work best. Make sure your skirt hems don't stop at the widest part of your leg. Stick to neutral-toned hosiery, or slightly darker colors—never pastels or off-white shades.

HEAVY WOMEN

I have been told by salespeople in shops that specialize in clothes for very large women that often these women put off a shopping trip until they are positively desperate for something to wear. They keep telling themselves that they are going to lose weight, and that they will wait and buy clothes when they are thin. A year later these women come back; they are the same size but still have nothing attractive to wear.

If you are overweight—whether ten pounds or a hundred—resolve to concentrate on the here and now. Don't procrastinate. Buy clothes that fit you today in attractive colors and fabrics. A large woman needs to spend money on the best quality she can afford: A good cut plus good quality fabric will give her the most flattering look possible.

Since the larger woman is more prone to wrinkling her clothing, she should buy fabrics that look natural but contain sufficient polyester or nylon so they will resist creasing. Heavier women should look for soft material in dresses and blouses, material that moves gracefully rather than material that stays stiff and unnatural. Keep these recommendations in mind as you shop:

- Fit is critical. If you need to buy a larger size than you have been wearing, then do so. More people will see the flattering fit than the label with the size on it. Half-sizes are often the answer for large women; they are cut larger in the bust and stomach. The final test is how a garment looks and feels on you, not the size.
- The fine details of fit are worth paying attention to: Be sure the jacket doesn't pull across the shoulders or around the armholes. A large-size skirt should have some elastic in the waist for ease.

This is a bulky, overly layered look that makes this woman appear extremely wide. The large belt and unfitted white jacket shorten her body proportions. White shoes are better left for casual wear.

When a woman's waist is defined either by a fitted jacket or a belt the look is slenderizing. The same color, shoulder to hem, makes her appear taller and thinner, too. Her hair is restyled off her shoulders; this gives her a much crisper appearance. Her open-toed pumps are a business shoe with a little more flair than plain pumps.

■ Select from these basic styles: skirted suits purchased as separate pieces for a better fit; classic jackets cut to flatter your individual size (shorter jackets for short women, to give them the benefit of a longer leg look, and longer jackets for taller women); A-line or dirndl skirts, rather than straight styles; blouses or dresses with a defined waist; and thin leather belts.

- Choose solid-colored jackets and dresses with small prints. Avoid any sharp contrast in color and texture, especially if you are short. Stark contrasts, such as a red jacket, cream-colored skirt, and black hosiery will chop your body visually into thirds and add extra pounds to each part.

- Look for small details elegantly executed: small covered buttons, small pointed collars, narrow vertical pintucking, narrow stitched-down pleats on skirts, small foulard prints, and narrow belts.

- Avoid the unbelted sack look that makes it too obvious you are hiding something. A dress with some definite shaping will be more flattering.

- Avoid lots of ruffles, lace, and flounces; bulky accessories like large stuffed purses or long, flowing scarves; large prints or too many bright colors; horizontal stripes; puffy sleeves; princess-line dresses; patch pockets; and uneven hemlines due to the tummy or derriere.

- Wear flattering colors, especially around your face, but keep jewelry and accessories simple, so you won't jingle and jangle.

SHORT WOMEN

You want particularly to avoid looking fragile or little-girl-like. Choose clothes that will give you a sense of substance and presence.

- Stick to solid colors, and don't break up your line with a sharply contrasting jacket and skirt. You may want to tone your hosiery, just slightly, to match your hem color.

- Stay away from pastels, except in small doses. They will make you look juvenile.

- Simple, clean lines will work best for you. Stay away from exaggerated details such as heavily padded shoulders, large prints, or flounces.

- If you have trouble finding clothes that fit well, check out the junior departments and even the girl's department, especially for blouses and other separates. You should find the selection good and the costs

Small women must be very careful not to clutter their appearance. This jacket is too big and too long. It is also too casual for most industries. The skirt cuts her calf at its widest part and the black ankle straps widen and shorten her legs.

A well-tailored suit styled without a lapel gives a very clean look. A soft dirndl camouflages a tummy or hips. The asymmetrical closing on the blouse, with small gathers and covered buttons, makes this a very versatile business blouse.

lower. Just be sure you don't emerge with a cute little junior high, prom queen look.

- Glasses, even if you have 20/20 vision, will add credibility and substance to your face.

TALL WOMEN

If you have height, you have very few limitations on what you can wear. Your body will be able to show off the lines of any style. Just make sure that everything is long enough—hemlines, sleeves, jacket length. Never wear anything that looks skimpy. Here are some other recommendations:

- Avoid heels that are absolutely flat for business. Choose a medium heel for a balanced look.

A short, skimpy jacket on a tall woman makes her appear to have outgrown her clothes. The sleeves are too short and the jacket should be longer. Her scarf clutters her look. The slit in her skirt is too revealing and will be an annoying problem when she sits. Her hair appears unkempt and straggly.

The most powerful and authoritative look for a woman is a matched, skirted suit in a dark color. But this look has been feminized by pairing it with a print blouse, pearl earrings and necklace, and a small pocket scarf.

- You can wear double-breasted jackets well if you aren't heavy in the midsection.

- Don't wear the hacking jacket style (a curved rather than square bottom with a higher waist), because it will make you look short-waisted and your legs will seem out of proportion.

- Don't wear the same color blouse, jacket, and skirt. That combination is too much of the same color over too long an area. A contrasting belt is a good method for stopping the eye in the middle.

- Don't overdo the authoritative look. Too much black or navy on a tall woman can be overwhelming.

- If your waist is well-proportioned, wear wider belts.

- Bring along a tape measure when you shop so you won't waste time trying on garments that are too short. Know your arm, leg, and neck-to-waist measurements.

- Jewelry pieces should be larger on a tall woman so that the entire look is well-proportioned.

□ 8 □

TINKER, TAILOR, CLEANER: ALTERATIONS AND CLOTHING CARE

Nearly all men's suits and a great many women's suits require some type of alteration. Even women's dresses and men's shirts may need some changes to ensure a good fit. An experienced tailor or seamstress is a godsend, and often spending a little money on alterations will upgrade a garment from a mediocre outfit to a very smart one.

It is important to know that alterationists are not miracle workers. They cannot stretch a size 38 regular suit to fit your 42 long frame, nor can they cut down a size 12 for a size 8 figure. Alterationists can "alter" the fit of the garment and tailor it to your particular body. There should never be any indication that changes were made.

There is a vestige of sex discrimination in the way alterations are charged. In most quality men's stores, there is no fee for very simple changes such as hemming or cuffing trousers or lengthening or shortening sleeves. But there generally is a charge for more complicated adjustments. In most women's stores, on the other hand, you can expect to pay for everything, even a simple hemming. There is some evidence that this discrepancy will eventually disappear, but it is more likely that men will begin paying for their alterations than that women will get them free.

Part of the reason for this cost discrepancy is that men's clothes are more easily altered than women's. The fabrics have traditionally been heavier, and are less apt to show signs of stitching and restitching. The lines of men's clothes generally tend to be simpler, lending themselves more readily to adjustment. A good rule of thumb is that if the alterations cost more than forty or fifty dollars, you are probably expecting too much.

Reasonable alterations for women's clothes may include lengthening or shortening the hem or the sleeve, letting side seams in or out, taking in or letting out the waist, narrowing lapels, replacing the buttons on a suit or dress if they do not match the fabric, and redoing the zipper or fasteners. Anything more complicated may cause trouble and add considerable expense to the price of the outfit.

Some women learn how to do simple hemming themselves. If you are sure of your skills with a needle and thread, you can save some time as well as money, but don't ruin a ninety-dollar dress for the sake of saving ten dollars.

Typical Alterations

COLLAR

LAPELS

WAIST

BUTTONS

POCKETS

SLEEVE LENGTH

SIDE SEAMS

SKIRT OR TROUSER LENGTH

A woman can have alterations done on a suit jacket, skirt, raincoat, or topcoat and on some dresses—although dress alterations, beyond the very simplest, ought to be approached with care, since the lighter fabrics may show the signs of restitching. It is not practical to alter most women's blouses, because this adds considerably to the cost and the changes will probably show. Most customized shirt shops are also selling blouses for women, should you be a difficult size to fit.

Men's suits, unless they come off the rack at Discount City, will need at least to have the pants hemmed or cuffed. The sleeves on the jacket may also need some adjustment. The waist can be taken in or let out and lapels and trousers widths can be cut down. The waist on a man's trousers may have to be let out or taken in, but this should involve no more than one to one and a half inches or you will ruin the lines of the pants and end up with a poor fit. Often the collar on a jacket needs to be lowered; occasionally it needs to be raised. These are all relatively simple, straightforward alterations that any competent tailor should be able to accomplish with ease.

A man can have alterations done on jackets, blazers, trousers, and even on a topcoat or raincoat. Ties can be narrowed down to a classic width of about three inches. Shirts can be taken in on the side, and the sleeves can be shortened; any more than that and a man is much beter off having his shirts custom-made or taking the time to try on a number of different ready-made brands to find one that fits around the collar and the sleeves.

However, it is risky to undertake any alteration involving the shoulder seam on either a man's or a woman's jacket. This is one place where the garment should fit with no changes. The shoulders, especially ones with padding, are a very difficult area to alter and you may not be pleased with the results, regardless of your tailor's expertise.

YOU AND THE TAILOR

If alterations are needed for a man's suit, request that the tailor, who will be doing the work, do the actual fitting, marking, and pinning. In large men's departments, each tailor or seamstress has a specialty and stays with one alteration—like raising or lowering collars—so it is conceivable that your suit may pass through three or four different hands. However, the initial fitter will have to understand and translate all your changes correctly, so you want an experienced person. A good salesman in a top-quality men's store can guide you during the selection stage about what alterations are possible; but it should be the tailor, not the salesperson, who actually *fits* the suit. A good tailor will measure both arms and both legs, and will not assume that every male body is symmetrical; in fact, very few are.

Be sure to inquire ahead of time about alteration costs, and get a definite commitment on the date the garments will be ready. Know the store's policy on improperly done alterations—a good store will redo them until the fit is right.

When you go to pick up your altered garment, don't leave the store without trying it on. If you are not satisfied, this is the time to say so. If you have your suit dry cleaned for the first time and the fit changes, go back and have the alterations redone. There should be no additional charge.

YOU AND THE SEAMSTRESS

Unfortunately for the woman shopper, department and specialty stores do not commonly have an in-house alterations department. Some of the better ones may have them, but more often than not you will be on your own. This means there is a greater risk attached to altering women's clothes than men's. Once you have paid for your garment and taken it out of the store to your own alterationist, the store is out of the picture, even if you are using a seamstress the store has recommended. This is a good reason for keeping women's alterations simple and for using someone whose work you are familiar with. Don't take your three-hundred-dollar suit to someone new. If your suit is ruined, you may get nothing except an apology.

ATTENTION TO DETAILS

Alteration reminders:

- When you are having alterations done, take the opportunity to add some personal details—a small inside jacket pocket for business cards, an extra flap and button sewn on the side pocket where the wallet goes; a monogram on the inside of the jacket.

- Be sure that all seams are at least one-half inch wide for future alterations, in case your size changes. Ends should be bound so they don't fray.

- Top-stitching, always in the exact same color as the suit fabric, gives a more formal look.

- Suit buttons should be sewn on with a shank of thread separating the button from the material, so the strain won't tear the fabric. This is a task for a knowledgeable seamstress, not a do-it-yourselfer.

- Trouser bottoms should be approximately nineteen inches around (based on a size 40), the same as the knee measurement.

- Always keep any extra fabric from the bottoms of trousers, sleeves, or skirts. If you ever get a cigarette burn or a moth hole in your suit, you can take the extra fabric to a professional reweaver.

- Some men ask for only three buttons on their jacket sleeves, simply because the discount outlet suits are all sporting four buttons.

- Individuals who perspire heavily should have underarm shields sewn into their jackets to protect the fabric.

RESTYLING

Even if you succumbed to some "high-fashion" details, an out-of-date suit is not necessarily a lost cause. If the problem is wide lapels, on either

Restyling a man's jacket and tie: narrow lapels, tie, shirt collar and pockets

Restyling a woman's jacket: remove lapels and collar; narrow side seams and shorten jacket; change pockets

a man's or woman's suit, a good tailor can cut them down to the more correct three- to three-and-a-half-inch width for men and two and a half to three inches for women. Similarly, men's bell-bottom trousers or wide-leg trousers can be narrowed fairly inexpensively to nineteen inches. If the flaps on the pocket of a jacket are three or more inches, they can be cut down to a more classic two inches.

Another clever way to restyle a woman's suit jacket or blazer is to completely remove both the collar and the lapel, move up the pocket and shorten it. With a little additional shaping at the waistline, the "new" jacket is clean and sophisticated-looking, with a very different appearance from the old one.

A good tailor can even reverse the frayed collar of a very well-made suit—although this is likely to be an expensive undertaking. Several old master tailors, who have received their training in Europe, can literally turn a suit inside out if the fabric is good quality.

If you find a good tailor, appreciate him. Take him out to lunch, buy him a bottle of wine. But don't lose his phone number. He has the ability to give your off-the-rack purchases a custom look.

CARING FOR YOUR CLOTHES

The value you get from your wardrobe depends to a great extent on the care you give it. This means taking pains to hang and store clothes properly, following manufacturers' instructions for laundering or dry cleaning, and not over dry cleaning your clothes.

BEFORE YOU WEAR THEM

Before you put on a new garment, check it over carefully to see that there are no loose threads or pins left from the factory or the tailor. New shirts will show fold marks and should always be laundered before they are worn.

Delicate fabrics, like silk, can benefit from being treated with one of the apparel sprays on the market. This will give the material the ability to repel wet stains like water, coffee, and soda. Ties and blouses are especially susceptible to this type of staining. But these sprays will not work on caramelized sugar spots, solid food stains, ink, and dirt.

STORING YOUR CLOTHES

Hang your jackets, trousers, and heavy coats on curved wooden hangers in a well-ventilated closet that allows each garment some "breathing room." Everything else should go on plastic hangers. Wire hangers are not a good choice because they will leave marks. Wooden hangers are more expensive, but they are a once-in-a-lifetime investment. Make certain they are polished and sanded, with no rough spots to snag your clothes. Plastic hangers work well for shirts, blouses, and dresses; simple clip hangers work best for skirts.

Always air out each garment for twenty-four hours before putting it back into your closet. This is especially important for any of your wool and wool blend garments. It will also allow natural fibers to regain their shape after a wearing.

Your woolen garments, which are susceptible to moth damage, should be stored out of season in protective bags that let air in but keep moths out. If you use some moth protection, make sure the cure isn't worse than the disease—in other words, choose a product that doesn't have the characteristic "moth-ball" smell. Your dry cleaner will often provide storage space for out-of-season clothing at a reasonable charge, or you can request plastic bags that have a nice cedar-chest smell to repel moths and silverfish.

STAINS

Spot cleaning with a noncommercial preparation should be a last resort for stains. Many of these spot removers are harder to get out than the spots themselves.

Be very leery of home remedies, such as hair spray or soda water (a favorite on airlines), which are often recommended for spills or stains. They work occasionally but very often simply serve to set the stain. The best rule of thumb is to blot up as much of the spill as possible, then see how fast you can get to a good dry cleaner for an emergency treatment.

The hardest stains to remove are protein stains, perspiration, and ink. Once you get a perspiration stain on a silk blouse, it is likely to be permanent. The combination of perspiration fluids and deodorant chemicals is deadly to silk. If you stain a machine-washable fabric, try one of the commercial prewash sprays. They are quite effective, so long as you use them before the washing, not after.

HOME LAUNDERING

One of the blessings of man-made fibers and many of the blends that incorporate them is that they are so easy to care for. Many can be machine washed and dried and still look fresh for a long time.

But don't push your luck. If a garment is labeled "hand wash only," then spend the time washing it out by hand. If the manufacturer's label stipulates "drip dry" or "line dry," then do so. In fact, many washable items, especially undergarments, dresses, and blouses, will benefit from line drying rather than being put in a dryer. Squeeze very gently with a towel to remove excess water, then hang them inside on a padded hanger, somewhere where they can literally "drip" dry.

When you do use the dryer, leave clothes in for as short a time as possible. Don't leave your silk lookalike blouse in for sixty minutes while a load of bath towels is drying. Take a tip from the good professional cleaners and don't stuff your washer or your dryer: That promotes wrinkling. Use maximum water levels and small loads. Remove clothes from the dryer promptly and put them on hangers.

Sheet-type fabric softeners not only take static electricity out of your garments as they are drying, but most will also remove wrinkles. If you leave a garment in the dryer for too long after the cycle ends and you want to get rid of the wrinkles, simply put the garment back in the dryer for a few minutes with a damp towel. This will take care of most of the wrinkles without necessitating another run through the whole wash and dry cycle.

Most garments require some finishing or pressing, even the ones marked permanent press. Know all the vagaries of your iron and its temperature settings, so you don't use too much heat and ruin the fabric— particularly if it has a polyester content. Be very careful when you are ironing a lapel. Often there is glue holding it together and a very hot iron will bubble it.

PROFESSIONAL LAUNDERING

Men's shirts look infinitely better if they are laundered professionally and finished with a light to medium starch. If the shirts are all-cotton this is essential; without starch, they will wilt by midday. A little starch will help even cotton and polyester blends stay fresher longer.

Heavy starch, however, is not advisable. It will shorten the life of your shirts because the fibers will crack, break, and fray anyplace the fabric is folded over—collar and cuffs. Most dry cleaners that do shirts consider this part of their operations as a "loss-leader." They don't expect to make a great deal off the shirts because of the heavy labor cost involved, but they are willing to offer the service for the sake of the dry cleaning business it will generate.

DRY CLEANING

Good quality dry cleaning is the gentlest of all cleaning processes; even washable fabrics may require it to prevent a vivid color from fading. It keeps natural fabrics from shrinking and colors from fading. However, over dry cleaning will shorten the life of any garment—for example, a suit that should last five years appears worn out after only two.

In years gone by, the characteristic dry cleaning odor (which actually indicated that some of the cleaning fluid remained in the clothes) was a "status" smell. It indicated that you were among those savvy to this new cleaning process. But this is no longer true.

Regardless of whether the fabric is a natural fiber or a blend, a good dry cleaner should not leave your garment with a chemical odor, pocketlines, hem marks, or the imprint of buttons and other trim. Nor should the fabric look shiny after cleaning. Since a good dry cleaning should not take any color out of wool, or a wool blend fabric, it is not necessary to send both parts of a suit to the cleaners if only one piece is soiled. Even a good dry cleaning job, though, may destroy a jacket lapel if too much glue was used in the construction. In that case, it would be the fault of the manufacturer, not the cleaners, if bubbling occurs.

The agitation portion of the dry cleaning process really separates the good cleaners from the poor ones. The agitation time should be regulated separately for each garment. Five minutes is sufficient for a wool suit, but much less time is required for a silk blouse. A cleaner that throws all kinds of fabrics and colors into one cleaning load and agitates them uniformly is likely to harm your clothes.

When a garment is damaged by dry cleaning, it is usually a result of too much agitation, an improperly functioning filtering system that has allowed moisture to get into the fabric, or a chemical solution that has dried out the fabric. Sometimes damage is done in the finishing process, when the presses are too hot. Be wary of one-hour cleaners. They can't possibly separate, properly agitate, and press all the garments that come in within sixty minutes.

FABRIC TYPES AND CLEANING

Wool blends, containing a certain amount of polyester, actually dry clean more effectively than one-hundred-percent natural fibers. The polyester content will facilitate the removal of stains. For finishing, a steam and pressure process is better for all fabrics than the hot pressure process.

Although wool responds beautifully to the dry cleaning process, many people actually overclean it. Every time dry cleaning is performed on a garment, the chemicals slightly deteriorate the fibers. Wool or wool blend suits generally only need dry cleaning three or four times a year if they are aired for twenty-four hours after each wearing. After this airing, the fabric will usually go back into its natural shape and odors will disappear. The exception to thrice-a-year cleaning would be a very light-colored or stained garment, or one that has a persistent odor even after a good airing.

Silk is the hardest fabric to clean and, thus, the most expensive. Some white or pastel-colored silk blouses can be safely hand-laundered, but colored silk is not colorfast. This is why dry cleaning is a better choice for silk. A good cleaner will use a mineral oil replacement on silk to bring back its lustrous appearance after the cleaning process. A silk lookalike, though, may actually come out better if you hand-launder it at home and then bring it to a cleaner for final pressing.

Men's ties do not fare well at the cleaners. Because they are cut on the fabric bias, ties do not respond well to flat pressing, which most cleaners utilize. If your cleaner has a special tie form, the results may be better, but a tie that has been pressed will never have the rolled edges it once had.

If your suit looks limp, simply have it pressed and skip the cleaning until it needs it. Quality pressing will not damage any garment.

SPECIAL CAVEATS

- Coin-operated, do-it-yourself dry cleaning is risky. You have no way of knowing the cleanliness of the cleaning fluid, nor can you control the agitation time.
- If you are traveling, be careful about having cleaning done at a hotel. You are better off investing in a steamer that you can carry in your suitcase or, simply, taking your more wrinkle-resistant garments along with you. If you wrap items in tissue paper or plastic bags before putting them in your suitcase, they will resist wrinkling.

FOR MEN:
HOW TO BUY A SUIT

Men have the advantage over women when it comes to business dressing in that the standards of men's wear, with a few painful exceptions like the leisure suit, have stayed relatively stable. The actual cut and styling of conservative men's suits has changed very little over the last four decades. Men's clothing has traditionally been designed to convey a certain sense of substance and solidarity. And men's clothes, in general, are designed to be more comfortable and ultimately more flattering to more body types than are women's clothes—many of which look good only on toothpicks.

Even the more limited selection of colors and styles works in a man's favor: It is harder for a man to make a mistake. But if a man does make a mistake in selecting a suit, it's going to be an expensive one, probably costing a minimum of two hundred to five hundred dollars.

So it pays to approach such a purchase with knowledge.

HOW MANY AND WHAT KIND

A man needs a minimum of five appropriate suits for a business wardrobe, to allow for proper rotation and airing-out between wearings. Unlike

Don't wear a jacket from one suit with trousers from another.

a woman's suit, a man's suit cannot be broken up so that the trousers are worn with other jackets or sportcoats. Similarly, the jacket cannot be worn with odd slacks. You will probably want to fill in your wardrobe with a blazer or sportcoat and several pairs of slacks for those times when you need a less formal look.

Blazers are a good choice in solid navy or camel, or in a tweed or herringbone pattern. Blazer and trousers should always contrast; they should never match. That is one of the reasons why most blazers are manufactured in a heavier fabric than suits. The look is for contrast—both in color and texture.

A plaid blazer is too sporty for business, so save it for a football game. Solid color trousers in khaki, gray, or navy are good choices, but avoid plaid slacks—they are too preppy.

The best suit colors are navy, medium blue, tan, and all shades of gray. Brown is a color that demands caution. A lot of people have a negative reaction to it, and it can easily look cheap. If you like brown, don't select solid colors. Use it in a tweed or herringbone, and save it for more casual looks. (See Chapter 6.)

The darker the color the more clout it ascribes to its wearer. The exception is a black suit, which should be reserved only for formal wear. A subtle pinstripe added to the navy is the maximum "power" look for a man, but a solid navy is more versatile and probably a better choice if you are starting your wardrobe from point zero. Pinstripes always upgrade the appearance of a suit in terms of power; they should be subtle and not too wide. (Refer to Chapters 5 and 6 for more information on color and fabric.)

For your core wardrobe of five suits, stay with lightweight to medium weight wool blends that can be worn year-round. They are easy to care for and do not wrinkle easily. You will also find the best suit selections in the blends.

Once you have established your five-suit and blazer core wardrobe (see page 54), then you can work your way up to a wardrobe of eight or ten active suits or blazers. This is the point at which you might want to add a few seasonal suits. If you live in a cold climate, a heavy winter flannel would be a good choice. If summers in your city are very hot, select a cotton poplin or pincord.

A good wool or wool blend suit, properly cared for, will remain in your active business wardrobe five to seven years. A good suit will look pretty much the way you bought it for the first two or three years; after that it may show some wear but will still be quite serviceable, especially if you spend the time to have it professionally pressed frequently.

The amount of hand stitching, as opposed to gluing or machine stitching, has a great deal to do with determining the cost of the suit. When the collar and lapel are stitched by hand, the cost of the suit will increase. If the lapel is glued to the inner lining and the stitching is done on a machine, the suit will be less expensive. Hand-stitched collars and lapels will make a suit fit much better, since it will mold itself to the body better.

STYLING

Unless you are in a very fashion-conscious industry, stay away from the tightly cut European-styled suits with high armholes, very defined waist, two back vents and variations in lapel widths. Any look that varies greatly from the standard three- to three-and-one-half-inch-wide lapels is likely to become dated very quickly.

European cuts are rarely flattering to any but the slimmest bodies. Nor does the "fashionable" European appearance convey the All-American male look that is still the best one to take with you into American business.

Classic suit jacket styles are two-button, three-button, or double-breasted. The two-button is a better choice than the three-button style. A double-breasted blazer or jacket is actually the only jacket that is always

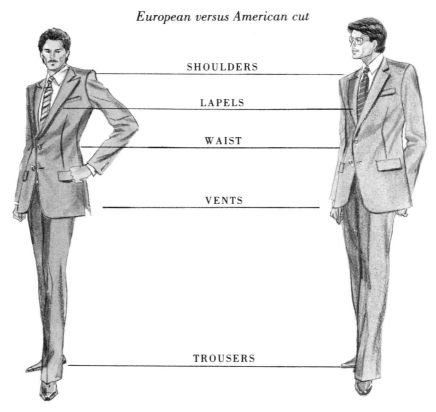

European versus American cut

SHOULDERS

LAPELS

WAIST

VENTS

TROUSERS

Incorrect

Correct

worn buttoned. For this reason, it conveys a formal look. Double-breasted styles are best worn by men who are tall and thin. Properly fitted, they can look quite elegant, but they add seven layers of fabric across the front, so the man wearing them must be slim enough to wear that much extra material.

Before you make a purchase, regardless of your price range, try on expensive suits to get an idea of how the look, feel, fabric, styling, and detailing all work together. Then try and duplicate these qualities in a less expensive line, if you can't spring for the "champagne" suit. Good fabric should be the number-one criterion.

If cost is a consideration, buy the lower-end line from a quality manufacturer or store, rather than the high-priced line at a discount or cut-rate store. Reputable stores have to maintain certain standards in everything they sell, especially if their name appears in the label.

FITTING THE SUIT

Above all, a suit must be comfortable. If it doesn't feel good, it won't look good. If you have a nice-looking suit that hangs unworn in your closet, chances are it is not comfortable. It's a good idea to know what alterations can and cannot do to the fit of the suit. Generally, alterations can lengthen or shorten the pants and the sleeves, adjust the waistline up to one inch either way, and raise or lower the collar. Usually shoulder size cannot be changed and a size 40L cannot be made into a 38R.

Forty dollars is a reasonable ceiling for alterations; any more than that and you're probably spending too much. (For more thorough information on alterations, see Chapter 10.)

When you are trying on a suit, try on each piece separately, then try them all on together. If it is a three-piece, see how the vest and trousers look together and then check the jacket and trousers without the vest.

SUIT JACKET AND BLAZER

Take it from the top. Check the collar. It should fit snugly around the neck and should not stand away from it. The lapels, three to three and a half inches wide (depending on your height), should lie flat on the chest. The peak of the lapel should not curl up or under. Shoulders should look natural, with only a slight bit of padding. The shoulder seam should hit just at the edge of the shoulders; it should not hang over and protrude and neither should the seam be so short that the armholes cut underneath the arm.

The back of the jacket should fit smoothly, with no wrinkling or buckling. Armholes should be loose enough to allow you to move freely and comfortably, but they should not be so large that you appear to have no shape. The back should have a center vent. Side vents are reserved for slender men who are in fashionable industries. No other obvious detailing is advisable.

If the suit is patterned, check seams and armholes to make sure the patterns match. The narrower the stripe, the easier to match at the seams and the richer the look.

The jacket should be long enough to cover the buttocks, and the sleeve should cover the wristbone and hit the top of the hand where the arm is bent. The standard four-and-one-half-inch measurement from the end of the thumb is not always a reliable guide. The sleeve length should cover the wristbone.

The jacket must fit, not simply hang. It needs to have a shape and follow the lines of the body. That is the reason why natural fabrics and good-quality blends look best. They are simply better able to mold to the body than one-hundred-percent man-made fabrics.

A suit jacket should have inside flap pockets; a blazer may have outside patch pockets. Blazers for business wear should not have elbow patches. A suit jacket or blazer should have at least two buttons on each sleeve, and these should match exactly the color of the suit.

A suit should have horn or good quality plastic buttons, but never brass

Suit jacket

Blazer

ones. A solid blazer usually has metal or brass buttons, and a tweed or herringbone jacket may have leather ones.

Some manufacturers skimp on the buttons to save money; but an easy solution is simply to have the tailor at the store replace the buttons for you; it should be done at no additional charge. A good tailor will always leave a shank of thread between the fabric and the button to facilitate buttoning and unbuttoning, rather than sewing buttons flat to the material. This also prevents ripping the fabric.

BUTTONHOLES

Buttonholes are an important detail, even though they are largely decorative. Men's suit jackets and blazers—with the exception of the double-breasted style—are rarely worn buttoned, yet buttonholes must be well and tightly sewn, whether they are on the front of the jacket, the lapel, or the sleeve. The slit buttonhole, which is often on the jacket lapel, allows a man to wear a flower in his buttonhole without having to pin it. However, flowers in lapels should be reserved only for those who have the élan to carry off the look. Or for the groom and his best man.

Functional sleeve buttonholes come only on custom-made or made-to-measure suits. Even then the main reason is to distinguish them from ready-to-wear styles, on which functional buttonholes would make sleeve alterations virtually impossible.

VESTS

Vests add a formal note to a suit, giving the maximum look of authority. They usually add a minimum of sixty dollars to the cost of the suit. The real purpose of a vest is to ensure that you don't lose your professional look when you shed your coat, and the idea is sound. In general, vests are a matter of personal choice—although wearing one in the summer months is probably masochistic. They are also a matter of proper body type.

A vest should be long enough to cover the waistband of the trousers. No shirt material should ever show between the vest and the trousers. A vest should fit snugly but not be tight. All the buttons, except the bottom one, should be buttoned, and the vest should be sufficiently roomy so that the buttons don't pull. The vest should always be made of the same fabric as the suit and should never be reversible.

Since vests add considerably to the cost of the suit, many manufacturers are not including them. However, if you are buying from a good store and desire a vest for a two-piece suit, ask the salesman whether a vest can be ordered from the manufacturer. If the factory still has the fabric, it may be possible for you to get the vest for stock price rather than paying a custom fee.

If the suit is a plaid, even a subtle plaid, don't wear a vest. That is simply too much pattern. Vests may have two or four pockets: four is preferable. Vests do not look good on men who have protruding stomachs or on men who are very short. Properly fitted, though, vests can be quite slimming.

TROUSERS

The waistband on a pair of trousers should always hit the wearer at the waist, not on the hips. The button at the top of the trousers should hit a man at his navel, to ensure a proper fit. When the waistband is worn too low, the crotch also hangs low, giving a comical, Charlie-Chaplinesque look. Some men like to kid themselves into thinking they have a size 34 waist rather than a 38, just because they wear their trousers under their stomachs. Their clothing would look and feel much better in their correct size. The crotch should be as high as is comfortable, but never too tight. Trousers should measure about nineteen inches around the knee and the same around the bottoms.

A slight break in the trouser over the shoe is preferable, but too deep a break will look sloppy and will make a short or heavy person look shorter or heavier. The bottom of the trouser should actually cover the top half of the shoe.

Trousers cuffs are pretty much a matter of personal preference. The idea of cuffs originated in England, where men would roll up their trousers when they encountered a dirty

Incorrect Fit   *Correct Fit*

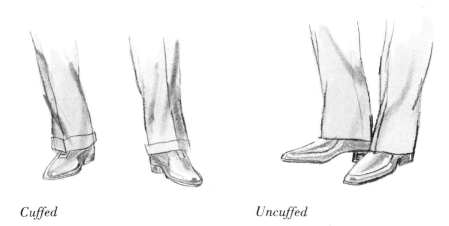

Cuffed   *Uncuffed*

street or went walking in the countryside. The cuff was then incorporated as a tailoring detail in English suits. But just as its origins were casual, the cuffed look today possesses a less formal air. Look at tuxedo trousers. They are never cuffed.

If you like the look of cuffs and their feel, use them on your less formal suits, like your tweeds, herringbones, and possibly tan. Leave them off a pinstripe or dark suit. Cuffs will shorten the look of a man's leg and should be avoided by any man shorter than five feet eight inches. A cuff will weight the bottom of your trouser leg and is likely to take some getting used to. Heels can catch more readily on a cuffed trouser than on a straight leg.

If you elect to wear cuffs, they should be about one and a half inches deep; a taller man can take a little more depth. Cuffed pants are always hemmed horizontally to the floor, never slanted, like a straight-leg trouser.

Trousers should be worn with a belt or suspenders, although many golfers seem to like the beltless look they find in their golfing clothes. Also, don't carry your wallet in your back pocket; this will destroy the lines of the trousers.

DETAILING

A suit jacket should be half lined with a matching color fabric, not fully lined. In fact, fully lined men's jackets are often the mark of a manufacturer who has something to hide in the way of workmanship. After several cleanings, the lining will probably hang out of the jacket if it is fully lined.

Lining that is brightly colored or contrasts with the color of the suit is ostentatious and in poor taste. Generally the best linings are man-made fabrics that have a "slippery" feeling. Rather than providing extra warmth, a lining is primarily for the purpose of helping the jacket hold its shape and making it easier to get on and off. Unlined or unconstructed jackets do not hold their shape well.

Unless they are custom-made, trousers are rarely lined. Even then, lined trousers are likely to be uncomfortable—hot in the summer, clammy in the winter. Occasionally a half lining, which comes down to the thigh, is a good compromise. If the outer fabric stretches and the lining shrinks, or vice versa, the fit will be compromised.

□ 10 □

AND THE SHIRTS AND TIES

Too many men who spend the requisite time and money buying good suits still regard shirts and ties as afterthoughts. The look of a five-hundred-dollar suit can be cheapened pretty quickly by the wrong shirt or tie. The right selections will do justice to the suit.

IF THE SHIRT FITS . . .

When you are buying a shirt, size is not nearly as important as fit. That you have been buying a 16 collar for years doesn't mean that's your correct size. Most men, in fact, actually wear their collars too tight. The result is that the shirt is uncomfortable, and there is a perpetual wrinkle in the band of the collar, which can be especially prominent in a button-down style.

It doesn't have to hurt to look good. If you find yourself undoing your top shirt button at every opportunity, try a collar that's a half inch larger than the size you've been wearing since you were in high school. You may be surprised at how much better you feel, and no one but you and your shirt salesman will know why.

A professional look demands long-sleeved shirts, even in the summer. Short sleeves simply look small-town, bush-league. The man wearing them looks unfinished. Long sleeves are also more versatile, in that they can be worn year-round. The correct sleeve length is the one that puts the bottom of your shirt cuff either level with the bottom of your jacket sleeve or showing one-quarter to one-half inch below the sleeve. Whether the cuff shows is entirely a matter of personal preference, but a sleeve that's too short makes you look somewhat vulnerable, even poor—as though you couldn't afford a shirt of your own and had to borrow one from your kid brother. The rule of thumb is that a shirt that doesn't feel right doesn't fit right and, therefore, doesn't look right. And fabric, of course, will have a great effect on the feel of the shirt.

For all types of business wear, the only real choices are one-hundred-percent cotton or a cotton-polyester blend. Certainly the most comfortable shirt is one that is all-cotton. It will breathe, move with you, and absorb moisture; but it will require professional laundering, including a light to medium starch. But I firmly believe that a relatively small amount of money spent each week on professionally laundered shirts is one of the best investments any businessman can make. The crispness of the collars and cuffs cannot be matched by even the best home job.

Cotton blended with Dacron polyester will require you to sacrifice a little comfort, but it will resist wrinkling better than one-hundred-percent cotton. Yet cotton and polyester shirts still need ironing for a professional look. A quick shake after taking them out of the dryer is not enough attention to detail; they need starch.

With blends, there is always a potential odor problem. A blend will hold perspiration, but an all-cotton shirt won't. A cotton blend shirt will often "pill" around the neck where your beard rubs against the material. This pilling is caused by the man-made polyester pulling away from the natural fiber. A man with a heavy beard should stay specifically with one-hundred-percent cotton.

If you buy a cotton blend shirt, be sure that the fabric's cotton content is higher than its polyester content: a fifty-five-percent blend would be the minimum combination to consider.

COLOR AND STYLE

Correct shirt colors for business wear are primarily solids—white, of course, and pale blue. A very thin pinstripe in blue or red is an acceptable alternative. White collars and cuffs on solid-colored shirts are a nice change but they are for less conservative industries. Ecru and pale pink fall into the same category; they are more fashionable and less conservative.

Avoid the real fashion colors like lavender or peach, unless you are in an industry—advertising, for instance—that tolerates more of a true fashion look. Save your plaids and dots—whether they are large or small, splashy or subdued—for casual occasions. Relegate the very broad stripes to your pajama tops.

Best shirt choice   *Acceptable alternatives*

Shirt collars are either straight or button-down. A button-down style gives a neat look and requires no collar stays. They were first introduced to America in the early 1900s and have become a mainstay for many businessmen. The button-down style works only in oxford cotton, never in flat cotton broadcloth. It also provides a slightly more casual look, and is less formal than the mat broadcloth. A button-down collar should never be combined with a French cuff, only with barrel cuffs.

Straight collars are more common and give a more formal look. They do require collar stays to ensure that they don't turn up at the points. This style collar goes properly with either a French or barrel cuff.

The collar of a shirt worn with a business suit should be about two and a half to three inches from the fold to the point. The spread of the collar—or the distance between the two sides of the collar at the widest point— should be no more than two and a half inches. However, a heavy man should decrease this by about three-quarters of an inch to make his neck appear thinner. A good conservative medium-width collar will be in proportion with your classic-styled suits and will complement your ties as well. Avoid the look of eagle wings flapping in the breeze that results from a too-wide collar or the unnatural narrow look.

Button-down   *Straight*

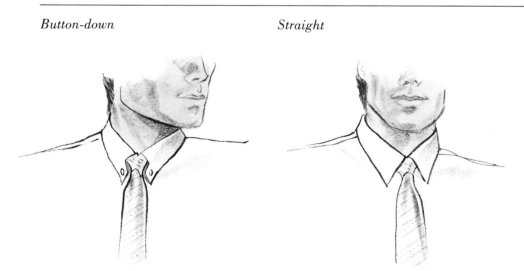

Barrel cuff   *French cuff*

Collar pins have a way of going in and out of style. They add a dressy note to a suit and crisp up a collar. If you choose to wear one, buy a shirt that has two small eyelets on the collar so the pin will appear to have a reason for being there. Or you may select a "clip-on" pin that is very tight and will stay in place. A real pin worn on a shirt that does not have special eyelets will leave holes.

Cuffs should be snug but still able to accommodate a watch nicely. The barrel cuff has two buttons to ensure a tighter fit. In better-made shirts there is also a button on the placket, the fabric surrounding the opening above the shirt cuff. The barrel cuff is less trouble than the French cuff, because it is "self-contained." But don't select a convertible cuff—one that either buttons or uses cuff links.

A French cuff is a very elegant detail on a shirt. Because it is more formal, it should not be worn with blazers. If you choose French cuffs, you will need a simple gold or silver cuff link—or as close to the real things as you can manage, but with no sparkling stones. The actual "link" types are the more elegant, better than the styles that clip in back.

CUSTOM-MADE SHIRTS

Some men can't find ready-made shirts that fit them well, so they opt for custom-made shirts. Other men simply enjoy the luxury of made-to-measure garments. If you decide to have your shirts custom-made, make sure you get your money's worth:

- Select French cuffs; they provide a dressy look and are becoming harder to find in ready-made shirts. This way your custom investment will appear truly custom.

- Select a neckband that flatters you. If you have a long neck, select a higher collarband of two to two and a half inches. If your neck is short, use a narrow band, and a quarter to one and a half inches.

- Leave off the pockets unless you actually use them.

- Make sure the tailor takes ten to fifteen different measurements to ensure a personal fit; otherwise, you might as well purchase ready-made shirts.

- Consider a subtle monogram on the left rib cage of your shirt—never on the collar or cuffs and never in letters taller than one-quarter inch.

TIES

A tie should pull your look together and add a necessary note of color. It should enhance, not startle. It should make a quietly eloquent statement about you rather than shout. Investing in four or five good-quality silk ties is one of the most inexpensive ways to upgrade your entire wardrobe without repurchasing all your suits. A tie has the ability to lift everything surrounding it. On the other hand, nothing will ruin a beautiful suit quicker than a gaudy, cheap tie.

A one-hundred-percent silk tie is the most appropriate choice for business. It is both versatile and elegant. Silk gives a very polished, conservative look and is correct in any climate, at any time of the year. However, a mixture of half silk and half wool produces a very beautiful tie well suited for cooler weather.

All-wool ties can only be worn in the winter. They give a more casual look and are better in solid colors, worn with blazers.

Linen ties are not a good value. The look is quite informal and resortlike, and linen can be worn only during hot weather. Linen ties wrinkle quite easily and in most industries are not appropriate.

Incorrect: short-sleeve shirt, wide tie that is knotted so it looks too short

Correct: long-sleeve shirt, tie hits middle of belt buckle

Stick to your natural fiber convictions when selecting ties. A Dacron polyester blended into the silk of a jacket is fine. Man-made fibers won't work in a tie. They will never knot as well as pure silk, all-wool or a blend of the two. Even when blended with silk, the man-made fabric will offer more disadvantages than advantages, at a very minimal price difference.

The smaller the knot in the tie, the more elegant the look; yet the knot should be large enough to fill the space at the top of the shirt. The four-in-hand knot is generally the best one. The Windsor knot, which is larger, was introduced by the Duke of Windsor to wear with his cutaway shirt collars. The space at the top button was quite wide, so he needed a very large knot to fill in the area. But today's button-down shirts and straight collars require a smaller, more precise knot. The half-Windsor is in between the four-in-hand and the Windsor and is sometimes needed to make sure the space at the top is filled. This can be a problem with very fine textured silk.

The traditionally styled tie, approximately three to three and one half inches across at its widest point, is the best choice to complement classically cut suits and blazers. Nothing dates you as quickly as last year's wide fashion tie with this year's fashionably narrow lapel. The proportions are wrong. So you are better staying with the classic three-inch tie to wear with your business attire. The exception might be a paisley tie, which should be slightly narrower to compensate for the "busier" pattern.

Bow ties, on the other hand, are correct only for formal wear or for an occasional fashion look. But because they can so easily make a wearer look comical, they are not good choices during working hours. They leave too much of the shirt exposed and can make a man look unfinished. Besides, very few people can tie a good bow-tie knot, and clip-ons, even the type attached to a band, are not acceptable.

PATTERNS AND COLORS

Subtlety is the key in choosing a tie pattern. The tie pattern and color should complement the suit and shirt. Never match your tie and jacket exactly. A navy jacket would not take a solid navy tie and, ideally, not even one with a predominantly navy background. A better choice would be a yellow or burgundy background with a small amount of navy in the pattern.

These are the best business choices:

Foulards are small, regular geometric prints with a very rich-looking Ivy League appearance. They are sometimes referred to as "neat" by specialty clothing stores because, in the strictest sense, foulard is a type of silk. This pattern is perhaps the best all-round choice for a business tie, as long as the print is kept very small in scale. Burgundy, navy, yellow and gray work well as background colors.

Stripes in a tie should be diagonal, since ties are cut on the bias of a fabric. This pattern is correct with nearly every type of suit and blazer. The stripes of the same color should be the same width. Two colors work well, with three as a maximum. Do not use multiple bands of color incorporating floral designs or patterns.

Dots can provide a nice look in a tie, as long as they are kept very tiny, almost pinpoints. Oversize polka dots make you look like a graduate of the Emmett Kelly School of Fashion. Small white pindots on a dark background are a particularly nice complement to a white shirt because they will pick up the crispness of the shirt. Generally, the dots should match the color of your shirt. Small dots look nice with either solid or pinstripe shirts.

Solid color ties, in dark tones of navy, burgundy, or beige, should be worn only with tweed jackets or camel's hair blazers when the desired look is less formal. Don't wear a solid tie with a solid shirt and a solid suit or you will miss the point of wearing a tie. It should add some interest.

Club ties, which incorporate patterns of ducks, hounds, or other insignia, are good only for a more casual look with blazers and light-colored suits. Usually good quality club ties are more expensive than other ties because the pattern is embroidered into the tie.

Paisley ties are usually worn slightly narrower than the conventional three inches and are more attractive when the pattern is subdued and the colors are rich. It takes a lot more searching to find a good paisley print than any other pattern. Paisleys can be included in a man's tie wardrobe but they should not be the mainstay.

Whatever color or pattern you select for your tie, *do not* buy a matching pocket handkerchief. That's amateur dressing. If you have the panache to wear a pocket handkerchief, it should be white or a solid color that coordinates with the tie and jacket.

LITTLE THINGS MEAN A LOT: ACCESSORIES FOR MEN

Accessories are a boon to any wardrobe, but particularly to a classically styled business wardrobe. Men can gain a lot of extra mileage from their clothing by buying proper accessories. Good-quality shoes, jewelry, and briefcases can upgrade any business look, just as ill-chosen accessories can downgrade it.

UMBRELLAS

Umbrellas should be discreet and functional; black or brown are the best colors. The collapsible styles are acceptable and convenient, especially if they fit into a briefcase. But save the golfing umbrellas for the golf course. It will help if you keep in mind that the only real purpose of an umbrella is to keep you dry when it rains. Status umbrellas are a waste of money; most umbrellas, no matter how humble or exalted their origins, come to the same end and get left in a bus, in a taxi, or in a corner at a restaurant. Put your money in less ephemeral items.

BRIEFCASES

A briefcase is a very important accessory. Aside from providing room for you to carry important papers and documents—or your lunch—it is a very powerful addition to your wardrobe. It stamps you as an important person, one with miles to go before sleeping.

You'll probably do better buying a briefcase at a large office supply store, rather than at a department or luggage store. Both selection and price will be better. If you are a regular patron of the store or if your firm is, you may even be able to negotiate a discount.

Leather is the preferred material for a briefcase, but prices will probably start at $150. For somewhere between $50 and $125 you should be able to find a good serviceable vinyl case. Don't, however, pay more than $125; beyond that you should be able to find something in leather that will be a much better value.

A good-quality vinyl case should last up to five years. But select one that resembles leather and look for these important details: actual stitching rather than embossing; reinforced corners; and a real leather handle that is reinforced with stitching.

Check the rivets on the handle to make certain they are firmly attached; check those that attach the hinges on the back of the case. If there are no rivets, the case is glued and will not wear well.

A leather briefcase should last you anywhere from five to ten years and will require a minimum of care. Glamorous-looking materials like eelskin, ostrich skin, or lizard are not good choices for day-in, day-out serviceability.

For an investment of two to three hundred dollars you should be able to get an excellent quality leather case. Look for thickness in the leather you choose: Very thin, delicate leathers will not wear well. All edges of a briefcase should be double-edged, with extra leather stitched on for additional strength. If the briefcase has hard sides, the corners should be rounded or have brass edges.

Belting leather is the most expensive and the longest-lasting of briefcase materials. It is thick and durable, but subject to spotting and staining. It is the most natural-looking of all the leathers because of the visible imperfections. Body oils will darken it, especially on a handle. If spotting bothers you do not select this kind of leather.

When you are making your selection, be sure your briefcase has a wooden case, rather than one made of cardboard, which rain will curl. If you carry a lot of papers, select a briefcase that has a four-inch thickness; otherwise, a three-inch thickness will serve you well, and will actually look better.

The best color choices are burgundy, russet, tan, brown, or for the most formal look of all, black. Lighter colors do not have the look of stability afforded by darker tones.

Hard-sided briefcases provide good protection for their contents, but if you try to overfill them, they won't close. Soft-sided cases are more versatile.

If you don't need a briefcase, it is perfectly satisfactory to go without one. In fact, a very young man may look better with a leather note pad.

SHOES

Shoes deserve number-one consideration in an accessory wardrobe. The most important thing is that they fit well and are comfortable. If your feet hurt from improperly fitted shoes, then nothing else will matter.

Leather is really the only choice for shoes. Vinyl looks cheap and is always uncomfortable; canvas or cloth shoes are too informal, as are suede or pigskin. Suede is also very difficult to keep clean. Patent leather is appropriate only as an evening shoe.

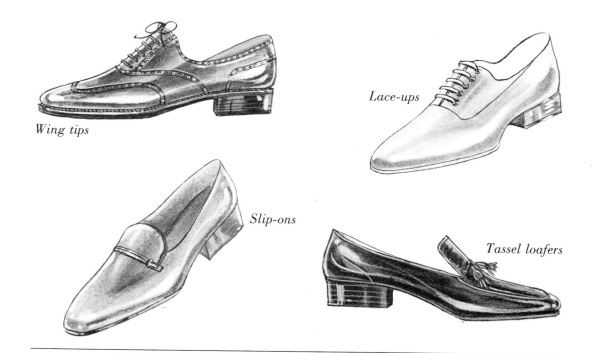

Wing tips

Lace-ups

Slip-ons

Tassel loafers

A lace-up or a slip-on style will serve you very well for business wear. A small bit of metal trim either across the vamp of the shoe or on the sides is a very good-looking detail. A tassel loafer is very appropriate in less conservative industries. However, a moccasin-style with very obvious stitching or a penny loafer is too informal, even though some men swear by them and have been wearing them since college. Very thin-soled shoes are best saved for evening wear; they won't hold up to everyday wear and weather extremes.

Although a wing tip is fine for daytime wear, it lacks the versatility of the other styles, because it cannot serve as an evening shoe. Also it is a very heavy shoe and should only be worn in colder climates. A more mature-looking man wears a wing tip far better than his younger counterpart.

Two-tone shoes are not acceptable for the office; nor are boots—with the exception of cowboy boots, which are appropriate in Western states or certain rural areas where they are routinely worn with business suits. The guiding rule should be whether you need them. If they are just for show, beware.

Men's shoes should be black, dark brown, or cordovan. Black will complement gray and navy suits; brown will go well with all shades of tan or beige. Never match a suit exactly to your shoes, but remember you do need a dark shoe color for proportion. White, pastel, or light-colored tan shoes are never appropriate for office wear. A shoe color should not be lighter than the trouser color. So white shoes worn with dark trousers, even if the trousers are casual, look ridiculous. People will see your feet before they see you. Lighter colors always make your feet look larger.

Shoes should be polished at least once a week, if possible by a professional. To extend the life of your shoes, always use shoetrees. They should be half trees made of cedar, which absorb odor. A half tree has wood only on the front, with a plastic handle on the back. The plastic will not break down the backs of shoes made of softer leathers. The exception to using a half tree would be for wing tips, which will take a full tree.

SOCKS

Socks should always be over-the-calf length, to avoid any visible expanse of hairy leg when you sit down or cross your legs, or any bunching at the ankle. The word on short socks is "no."

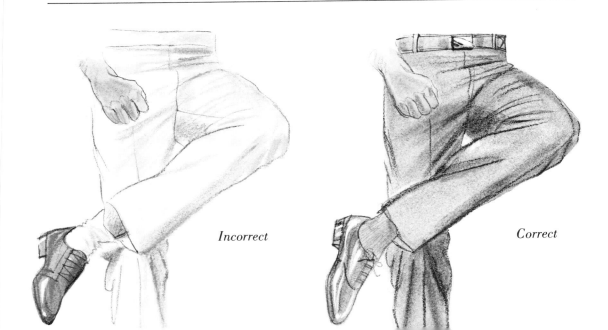

Incorrect

Correct

Brown, black, or navy will work with any color suit or trousers in your business wardrobe. You need at least ten pairs. White socks, of course, are appropriate only for sports or leisure wear.

Nylon or thin cotton are the best business choices; if you live in a cold climate, the cotton will provide more warmth. If the cold is severe you can buy sock liners, available at most outdoor or sporting goods stores, and wear those under your regular socks.

So-called luxury socks made of cashmere are an extravagance. They can actually be worn only once, since they will not clean successfully.

BELTS

Black, brown, or burgundy leather belts will enhance any suit or pair of trousers in your closet. Brown and burgundy are correct with tan and brown suits. Black is correct with all other colors. Choose a style one to one and a quarter inches in width, with a discreet brass buckle. No joke or fad buckles, please, or turquoise-studded souvenirs of your trip out West.

Beltless looks belong on the golf course; a business suit requires a belt or suspenders. Leather is the best material for belts, since vinyl will be uncomfortably hot in any weather, and fabric or rope belts are best saved for leisure wear. Choosing a belt color that matches your shoes is the safest way to make a selection.

COATS

You will certainly need a raincoat and perhaps, depending on where you live, also an overcoat. Either style should reach below the knees, or it will look too casual.

For your raincoat, choose a shade of beige or tan in a good-quality waterproof material. Pastel colors look too sporty and black and navy tend to appear rather dowdy; they are an old man's look.

The two best styles are the classic trenchcoat and the single-breasted. Both should have raglan sleeves. The trenchcoat should also be double-breasted and belted. The single-breasted style should have a fly front (a placket covering the buttons). Many styles come with a zip-out lining, and this often means getting by without buying a topcoat.

When it comes to overcoats, warmth is the major consideration. Choose one-hundred-percent wool or cashmere in a dark color, like navy, for maximum warmth and minimum cleaning. If you are exceptionally neat or don't mind the dry cleaning bills, a camel color is very rich-looking. The best style is single-breasted unbelted, with a fly front. An overcoat is an investment item. Given proper care, it should last as long as ten years.

GLOVES, MUFFLERS

Dark-colored leather gloves, fur-lined if you live in a very cold climate, are a good choice. Black and brown are the most versatile colors. A pair in each color gives you the ability to match your shoes with your gloves. Avoid knits for business. They look too much like schoolchildren's mittens. Scarves should be soft wool or cashmere for warmth, in a dark color or discreet plaid. Not only do they provide warmth, they also keep the neck of your coat clean, cutting down on dry cleaning bills.

HATS

Conservative accounting firms used to require the standard gray felt business hat—the fedora. Today, it is more a matter of temperature and comfort, because a great deal of body heat is lost through the head.

Caps are a more casual look but still very appropriate for business. They feature a bill in the front, rather than a brim all the way around. A good-looking wool cap is the preferred choice for most men, while the traditional fedora should be reserved for the more mature man. Always avoid any hat with ear flaps, except in sub-zero weather.

JEWELRY

A man's watch should be gold, silver, or a very good quality imitation. Keep the watch thin, tank, or oyster style, or use a pocket watch. Avoid thick, gimmicky-looking digital sports watches that tell you your heart rate and best jogging time. The watchband should be *leather*, not an expandable gold imitation.

Men's rings should be limited to wedding bands or signet rings—no more than one ring on each hand. Large, brilliant stones are off limits.

In seminars, I am often asked about fraternity insignia, such as those which frequently appear on men's college rings. I am always tempted to answer with an unqualified no, but it is obvious that many successful men—bank presidents and top executives—wear these rings, so I have been forced to reconsider. If you are in a familiar business environment in a place that is well known to you and if you feel comfortable wearing your fraternity ring, then wear it. But if you are in a strange environment or are traveling outside your familiar territory, you should leave it at home. The look is generally more acceptable in the South and Midwest, where there are large state universities with a multiplicity of fraternities. If you're a "hometown boy" doing business in a city where you went to school with half of the business establishment, then go ahead. But be aware that it is a somewhat provincial look—your Phi Delta Theta–stamped ring probably won't help you get a table at the Four Seasons in New York, even if they love you at home at Mae's Diner.

It's best to avoid lapel pins, tie tacks and tie bars altogether. Those that

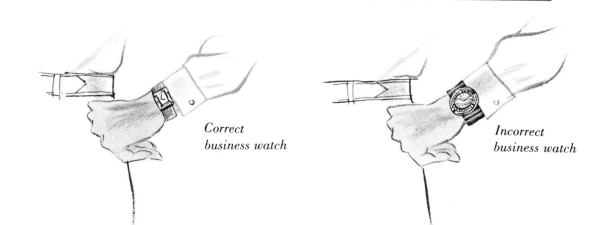

*Correct
business watch*

*Incorrect
business watch*

have some sort of fraternal or civic group significance should be saved for club-related activities. Visible religious medals are not a good idea; if you wear one around your neck, keep it a private matter.

To keep your tie neat and still avoid necktie jewelry, tuck the narrow end into the label sewn on the back of the tie.

Whatever you do, don't decorate yourself with gold chains or bracelets. The look says *gigolo*, and the older you get, the more ridiculous you will look. The over-the-hill swinger look won't win you many corporate clients.

HANDKERCHIEFS AND POCKET SCARVES

Handkerchiefs are functional and should be white linen or cotton. Make sure you have a clean one daily—several of them if you are in the throes of a bad cold. There is nothing less attractive than someone searching for a clean corner on a wrinkled, soiled handkerchief.

Pocket scarves wax and wane in popularity, and when they are "in," they can be very attractive. But the look takes some maturity and style to pull off. If you try it, select a subdued pattern on a dark background, a solid color, or white. Never match your tie with your pocket scarf. If you wear a navy patterned tie, then choose a solid navy for the pocket and make certain that only a small bit of the scarf shows, either tips or the fold. Silk or cotton are the only choices for a pocket scarf.

WALLETS

Your wallet should be made of good-quality leather, in black or brown color. It should not be allowed to bulge with anything—not even money. Carry it in your inside jacket pocket, never in your back pocket.

The preferred shape is the oblong "secretary" style, rather than the square "wallet" shape.

Incorrect

Correct

□ 12 □

LOOKING GOOD: MEN'S HAIR AND SKIN CARE

Good grooming, especially attention to hair and skin, is as important for a man as for a woman, perhaps even more so, since men don't have the wide range of camouflaging cosmetics and flattering hair styles available to them that women do. Most cosmetics manufacturers sell lines of men's cosmetics, but they are generally limited to soaps, scents, and shampoos. Outside of the entertainment industry, "real men" don't wear makeup.

FACIAL HAIR

Without a doubt, the most frequent questions we get from men at our seminars relate to beards and mustaches. Most of the men who ask if they can keep a beard or mustache can anticipate our answers, but they ask the questions anyway. However, the advice is unchanged: *The safest look for a businessman is a clean-shaven look*. Everyone reacts positively to this look; there is nothing to offend or appear comical. A clean-shaven appearance is the most universally flattering. It makes most men look younger, cleaner, more efficient, and more businesslike. Some business people have negative reactions to mustaches, and many more don't like full beards at all.

Certainly there are exceptions. Some young-looking men need the "maturity" a well-trimmed mustache gives them; others are so emotionally attached to their mustaches that they become personal signatures. However, a scrawny, sparse, or very light-colored mustache will not enhance anyone's appearance. Some men find their mustache grows in an entirely different color from their hair—sometimes red; this can look ridiculous. Foolish-looking mustaches are like fishy handshakes—instant turnoffs that seem to indicate a lack of character. A mustache too often gives a downward droop to a man's mouth, making him look perpetually gloomy or discouraged.

Full beards are especially risky. They are worn well by only a very small minority of the general male population. Contrary to popular opinion, a beard does require a lot of maintenance—clipping, shaping, pruning, shampooing, and peripheral shaving. The best reason to wear a beard would be if you have a very small chin or an undistinguished jawline; a beard might help normalize these traits and give your face a better shape. But the beard must be thick and extremely well-groomed.

Too often a beard is seen as a rebellion against authority or prevailing standards. So despite the fact that many men like to grow one to assert their virility—after a painful divorce, very often—every man who does should know the risks.

In "creative" professions, like the arts and advertising, and on college professors, beards may be tolerated and even accepted. The fuzzy look may inspire trust. Often people who work in social services, like counselors and rehabilitation officers, can wear them. They work well on psychologists, too. (Sigmund Freud had one.)

But a full beard is likely to reduce the credibility of anyone engaged in any occupation related to finance—banking, sales, insurance. Clients and customers wonder why you are hiding.

If you are bound and determined to have some facial hair, a mustache has wider acceptance than a beard. But keep it simple. No handlebars or waxed works of art. If you succumb to the urge to grow a beard, no goatees or Fu Manchus.

Whatever you are growing, give it three or four weeks. If it doesn't look lush and thick by then, shave it off: It will never look any better. And do have a professional hair stylist "style" your beard.

With facial hair, you must take particular care in eating. Wipe your mouth meticulously after every bite. Nothing is more disgusting to a dining companion than watching a piece of cole slaw caught in a hairy upper lip.

EYEBROWS

There's nothing particularly virile-looking about caveman eyebrows, the kind that grow together; so there is every reason to enhance your appearance by plucking them or undergoing electrolysis to remove the extra hairs permanently.

Some men remove the unwanted hair by shaving, but plucking is more effective and cleaner-looking. Heat and moisturize the skin and pluck in quick motions with a pair of sturdy tweezers so the procedure will not be painful.

NASAL HAIR

If you have hair growing from your nostrils, you should remove it by clipping rather than plucking, which will be too painful and irritating to the membranes in your nose. Use small scissors blunted at the ends. Hair that grows on your nose should be plucked.

MEN'S HAIR STYLES

Nothing can date you more quickly than long, bushy sideburns. Many men flirted with longer sideburns in the early seventies, but the pendulum has definitely swung back, so that only hicks and rock promoters wear them long and unkempt or, heaven forbid, growing into the corners of their mouths. Keep sideburns short, at least one half inch above the earlobe, never level with it. And keep them narrow.

Find a simple haircut and stay with it. You don't want to look like you just checked into boot camp, joined a punk rock group, or are retreating into the sixties.

An honest hair stylist will be your greatest asset for advice. Certainly a good cut and variation in style will enhance your good qualities; but get the advice of a professional before you make any major changes. And keep a standing appointment every three to four weeks for a consistent look.

KEEP IT CLEAN

Most men are well-advised to shampoo daily. This will not make the hair fall out; on the contrary, it will keep bacteria from forming on the scalp and ensure a healthier and thus more attractive head of hair. Use a good conditioner after every shampooing, especially if you play sports or exercise a lot. Most conditioners that you can buy in your neighborhood drugstore will work just fine—simply read the label and find the one that sounds best for your hair. Your hair stylist will probably be happy to recommend a brand for you, and probably even sell you one, too; but you will pay more for the "exclusivity" of the salon line.

A large part of the benefit from shampooing comes from the massaging of your scalp, so take time to massage. Never towel-dry your hair too energetically, since hair is at its weakest when it is wet. Blot it with a thick, absorbent towel and let the hair dry naturally until it is just damp. Then, if you like, use a blow-dryer to give it shape and fullness. But keep the dryer moving; holding it in one place will fry your hair.

If you need them, there are products on the market that can be applied directly to the hair before blow-drying to protect the hair shaft from the heat. Always finish off the blow-drying with cool air. This will help the style look better for longer.

COLORING AND CURLING

More and more men are taking advantage of the much improved color and curling processes that have been developed in recent years. If you keep the look conservative and redo it as often as necessary, you should be able to take some color and some "body" into the business world with you.

It has long been accepted that a little bit of gray at the temples makes a man look "distinguished," and indeed, often it does. But if the distinguishing gray hair appears before you are ready for it, or if it comes in an unattractive shade of yellow-gray, then don't hesitate to seek professional help. Once you are on the right track with your color, you may opt to do it at home for convenience.

Talk the idea over with your regular stylist and ask how many colorings he or she has done. If you know of colleagues who have had coloring, ask for recommendations. You may end up with one stylist for your initial coloring and another for your cuts. Often you may be better off with a stylist who specializes in women's hair than with one who has only male clients.

Avoid a deep, flat color that looks artificial. A softer shade than your own is advisable after the age of thirty-five, since your skin fades. You have three choices in terms of coloring. The first is a rinse—a bad idea if you perspire much, because it will streak down your neck. The second is semipermanent, which will last for about six shampoos and gradually wears out. The third choice is permanent hair color, which will stay in the hair until it grows out.

If you use a semipermanent color, you will need to have it redone frequently. If you opt for permanent color, it will need maintenance only at the roots every month or so.

RECEDING HAIRLINES AND BALDNESS

Be realistic about your hairline. Don't try to create something that isn't there. There is no single aspect of men's grooming that looks more self-conscious than a low part over the ear, with the remaining strands of hair left long to be wrapped across the head and sprayed into a helmet. No one is fooled.

Some hairpieces and toupees can work but I personally don't recommend them. If you want to buy one, you definitely need the help of a professional; and you should expect to pay a great deal for those that look good. Their biggest drawback is that the hair on them doesn't move. So they are always somewhat unnatural-looking.

Hair transplants are expensive and painful. You also must be willing to be bandaged for several weeks. But they are probably the most natural-looking and reliable method of regaining a hairline.

I recommend heartily that a man accept his hair quantity for what it is and concentrate on looking the best he can all over. Nearly all men experience some hair loss. It isn't fatal . . . to business or social life. Some very attractive bald or balding men who are clients of my company have become even more attractive by ceasing all pretense of having a full head of hair.

Baldness is nearly always genetically determined. The best thing to do is maintain a neat, well-trimmed hair style—working with whatever amount of hair you have.

SKIN CARE

Clean, healthy skin is an asset to a man, just as it is to a woman. Men's skin often remains younger-looking than women's, because daily shaving removes dead skin cells, along with whisker stubble.

Shaving is actually a very healthy process for most men. The problem comes with razor burn, which is an irritation caused by a residue of soap left on the skin, or when the hair becomes ingrown, a condition to which black and Latin men are more prone.

Ingrown facial hair deserves treatment by a dermatologist; but razor burn can easily be cured by changing brands of shaving cream, changing razor blades or simply remembering to rinse your face thoroughly after each shave. Whether you use a safety razor or an electric shaver is a matter of personal choice. The electric models have been improved considerably in the last few years, but many men, particularly those with heavy beards, feel that electric shavers don't give them as close a shave.

The swarthy, gangster look is not a good business one. Some men keep a small electric razor in their desk drawer so they can give themselves a quick shave if they are going somewhere from work.

If you suffer from acne or if your face is scarred from an earlier bout, consult a dermatologist. He or she can advise you on dermabrasion, which will aid in removing facial scars.

FOR WOMEN: HOW TO BUY A SUIT

The classically styled suits in your closet are the mainstays of your wardrobe, the true basics. They will provide the foundation for an effective professional look that will still leave you room for individuality. A well-cut, well-fitting suit can be accessorized into an office look without being frilly, authoritative without being dull.

A classic suit is versatile; the individual pieces can often combine with a jacket or skirt from another suit, and the jacket can be worn with dresses.

Because the suit is the beginning of a good business wardrobe, it deserves the most consideration and the largest dollar investment. A business suit should always be a skirted one, not a pantsuit. Trousers or pants for women are too casual to provide an effective business look. The suit you buy should be of the very best quality you can afford, because it should last at least three years, and probably longer. It is far better to have several suits that are worn over and over with different accessories than cheaper outfits that simply give variety and no quality.

SUIT JACKETS

Classically styled suit jackets are usually fully lined, with long, set-in sleeves. They should have no bust darts. If the jacket has buttons, they should be left unbuttoned—unless it is a double-breasted style. Classic jackets are not required to have a lapel. But if they do, the lapel should not be wider than three inches or narrower than two inches. A classic jacket will have either a center vent in the back, if it is more narrowly cut, or no vent at all, if it is a fuller cut. It should never have side vents.

SINGLE-BREASTED JACKET

This is the most formal and conservative of all the classic jacket styles for women, yet it is one of the most versatile. This jacket works well with nearly every skirt style. Characteristically, it has a simple rolled collar with three-inch lapels; a breast pocket and inside flap or vent pockets, as opposed to outside patch pockets; and matching buttons. Combined with a straight skirt, this style jacket gives the most conservative, most authoritative, and often the most slimming look.

The blazer is a variation of the single-breasted jacket, except that the pockets are generally on the outside, and the buttons on a blazer are usually brass.

NONLAPEL JACKET

This style gives a clean look that is slightly more fashionable than the single-breasted lapelled jacket. A nonlapel jacket is usually a shorter cut, a bit less boxy and better on shorter women. The closing is either an edge-to-edge front closing or a wraparound closing. If it is edge-to-edge, it should always have buttons, otherwise it will appear sloppy and home-made. A wraparound would not have buttons, but it should have a good quality belt.

If the bottom of the jacket is straight, it will appear longer. If it is curved, it gives the illusion that it is a shorter jacket; this is better for a shorter person who wants the length in the back but a leggier look in the front.

The jacket may have a breast pocket and flap or vent pockets on the hips, but it should not have a center vent in the back. The nonlapel jacket can take more detail—interesting blouse necklines, scarves, jewelry— because of its cleaner line.

DOUBLE-BREASTED JACKET

This style is most flattering to taller and thinner women, because it adds pounds to shorter frames. The double-breasted jacket may be collarless or have a two-inch to three-inch lapel. It comes with or without a breast pocket. Characteristically, it has inside pockets, flap or vent-style on the hips, and is made either with a vent in the back or with none at all. Unlike the other styles, the double-breasted jacket is always buttoned and it does have a more formal look. The double-breasted is also the most difficult to separate and wear with other skirts.

The two rows of buttons need to be fairly close together so they won't appear to widen the torso.

Edge-to-edge

Wraparound

Double-breasted

UNSTRUCTURED JACKET

This is the most casual of all classic jacket styles, but can still be well within the bounds of professional attire, depending on your business. It is usually cut longer and fashioned with an attached collar. It may or may not have buttons. There may be a breast pocket or patch pockets on the hips.

The cut for this jacket is fuller than that for the other styles, and it is more attractive in softer fabrics, as opposed to the hard finishes. There is no center vent in the back because there is no need for easement. The jacket will probably have gathers on the shoulders with set-in or dropped sleeves: Set-in always looks more formal. Often the sleeves have enough ease so that they can be pushed up for a more updated look. This style jacket is frequently unlined. Belting it will provide a more formal look.

*Unbelted
for a more informal look*

*Belted
for a more formal look*

VESTS

Vested suits for women float in and out of style. For that reason, it is smart to keep the vest even if it is currently unfashionable, because chances are it will be back. When vested wool suits are featured by the manufacturers, they are the strongest and most authoritative look, but they can become too mannish and overdone. If you are large-busted, you will probably have a very hard time getting one to fit properly, so it would not be a good choice. A woman's vest functions much like a man's; when the jacket is removed, there is still a feeling of being dressed up.

It is important to guard against a mannish or matronly look in vested suits; this works against a professional appearance. The best way to counteract a too-severe vested look is to pair it with a softer, feminine blouse style or accessorize it with a piece of jewelry.

Sweater vests are better on women than on men. In fact they can be businesslike when worn with a lapelled jacket and straight skirt. They need to be tailored and not in fluffy fabrics. The most enduring choices are the solid colors. Sweater vests are better when purchased a bit longer, so that they can be belted, thereby creating a more flattering look.

CLASSIC SKIRTS

Classic skirts will work well with most suit jackets and often with well-tailored sweaters. They will have back or side zipper openings. Button-front skirts are too casual for office wear, and are less flattering because they pull, stretch, and generally gape open. A classic skirt will usually have a one- to one-and-one-half-inch waistband, which is the most flattering, inside pockets, and a permanent hemline, which stops just below the knee at the thinnest part of the calf.

STRAIGHT SKIRT

This is the most formal of all the skirt styles. It hangs straight from the hips and has a minimum of four darts—two in front and two in back—for shaping; otherwise it will be too puffy. It should have a small kick pleat or vent in the back for ease of walking. An asymmetrical pleat in the front is an attractive detail. The skirt should not have side slits and it should never be tight and "cup" the buttocks.

This skirt needs to be worn slightly longer than other styles because it will "ride up" when you are seated.

MODIFIED DIRNDL

This cut is more fashionable than the straight skirt, and is flattering to most women because it camouflages the tummy area. It has a bit of fullness, with slight gathers usually in front and back. It doesn't usually require a vent or kick pleat because of the greater easement. The pockets are inside, running along the side seam, and are very flat.

PLEATED SKIRT

There are several different pleated skirt styles that are appropriate for suits, but sharp knife pleats are the most common. They have a wonderful feeling of movement. The most flattering look on most women is for the pleats to be stitched down to the center of the tummy so they don't pull open.

A pleated skirt may have flat side pockets that incorporate a side closing. It may also have an asymmetrical closing with a placket covering the button on the waistband.

A pleated skirt should have some man-made fiber blended in, so that the pleats can be heat set. The one-hundred-percent natural fibers cannot be heat set, which means paying extra at the dry cleaners for individual pleating.

A-LINE SKIRT

This is a very comfortable, easy-to-wear style that skims lightly over a woman's body and is safest for someone with larger hips and tummy. It is also a good choice for a woman who gains and loses weight frequently, because it has a lot of easement and is also fairly slimming.

There is no slit or kick pleat on an A-line skirt. It may have a large inverted pleat in the front. The best look is for the inverted pleat to be unpressed. An A-line has a tendency to look dowdy, so it needs interesting accessories.

THE KEY ELEMENTS

COLOR

A suit's color, fabric, fit, and proportion should all work together. The best basic colors for women are black, brown to camel, burgundy, blue to navy, beige to taupe, and all shades of gray. The darker the color, the more authority the suit will impart to the woman wearing it. In some workplaces, women need all the power support from their clothing that they can get. Navy, charcoal gray, burgundy, or black will serve well for occasions when more clout is needed. Beige, taupe, and medium-range blues will convey a friendlier authority.

Pastel suits may be worn—but on very limited occasions—if you are very confident and the situation doesn't require a powerful look. Pastels can also be very attractive on a more mature business woman in her fifties or sixties because of their softening effect. In entry-level positions and on women in their twenties, they will probably be a poor choice.

A white linen blend or winter-white wool suit can provide an effective look when paired with very classic accessories. But it will need to be dry cleaned every time it is worn—so double the price of the suit before buying it for a realistic assessment of the cost.

FABRIC

The best suit fabrics are wool, wool crepe, wool blends, cotton blends, linen blends, and silk blends. Adding some man-made fiber to a natural fiber is a good idea, since it provides wrinkle-resistance and will help a suit keep its shape. For year-round wearability, however, it is hard to beat a light- or medium-weight wool blend that allows your body to breathe, even in the summer.

It is useful to think in terms of *hard smooth* finishes, like a gabardine or worsted wool, or *hard nubby* finishes, like a silk blend. Both are more useful (because they can be worn more months of the year), than the softer finishes, like flannel (for cold weather only).

Some fabrics, no matter what their color or texture, are simply poor choices for business suits. Corduroy is one of them. It is too casual and looks worn-out too quickly. Velvet is too dressy, even as piping or detailing on a suit. Suedes, ultrasuedes, leathers, and clinging knits are inappropriate for business.

When pairing different fabrics, be very certain that the look works. Remember that the softer fabrics belong on top, the harder finishes on the bottom. For example, a tweed jacket is very good-looking when combined with a gabardine skirt. Some fabrics, though, can clash, just as colors can. Certainly a linen jacket would never work with a heavy wool skirt, nor a cotton skirt with a tweed jacket.

FIT

Fit is all-important in selecting a suit. Even when the fabric and color are correct, you should put the suit back on the rack if the fit is poor. Buying the parts of a suit separately is a blessing for any woman who is one size on top and another size on the bottom. It considerably reduces the amount of alteration required.

Suits should be altered only by a professional seamstress or tailor, unless you are very skilled with a needle and thread. The hemline of a skirt should be permanently set at the small bone underneath the knee, or the slimmest part of the calf. Some shoulder padding on the jacket is necessary for a smoother look and for a more appealing silhouette. Shoulder pads will make a woman appear almost as broad-shouldered as a man when she is seated, which can be a real asset around the conference table. Side seams, sleeve length, and width of lapels can be altered. Shoulder seams and jacket length should not be.

When buying a suit, it is always better to purchase one with a slightly looser fit; a too-tight fit will cheapen the look of any garment, regardless of the price. This also allows for a five-pound weight fluctuation.

When you find a style that works well for your body proportion, stay with it. Don't buy less flattering styles just for the sake of variety. You can vary your look effectively with blouses and accessories, but there is little that can be done if the suit itself is unflattering.

STYLING DETAILS

Since classic suits have such generally simple lines, each detail takes on importance. There are no ruffles or flourishes to hide anything.

Buttons, which appear on most classically cut jackets, blazers, and skirts, can make or break the look of the garment. Cheap, tinny, or contrasting buttons always detract from your outfit. Buttons should be functional rather than simply ornamental. The exception is buttons on jacket sleeves.

On a suit jacket, buttons should match the fabric exactly and be either horn or bone or excellent man-made imitations. The only exception would be good-quality brass buttons on a dark blazer. Most good clothing stores for women's clothes will replace unattractive buttons at no charge.

Zippers should be sewn in very flat and reach to the top of the waistband. Both zipper and lining should match the fabric exactly. Some skirts will have no zippers or buttons but will utilize a metal closure within the side pocket. This fastener should be sturdy and durable and not a delicate crocheted loop. The waistband will take a great deal of stress and it needs security.

Pockets should be the same color and fabric as the rest of the jacket or skirt; anything contrasting will look too busy and make it impossible to wear the separate pieces with anything else. Bust darts in the jacket indicate a cheaply made, poorly cut garment. Side vents, which add inches to the posterior, will date the garment very quickly.

Avoid buying a suit that has top-stitching in a contrasting color. It will cheapen the suit. As you are building your *core* of basic suits, also avoid any kind of contrasting color trim or piping. These types of details limit you when you combine the pieces with other separates.

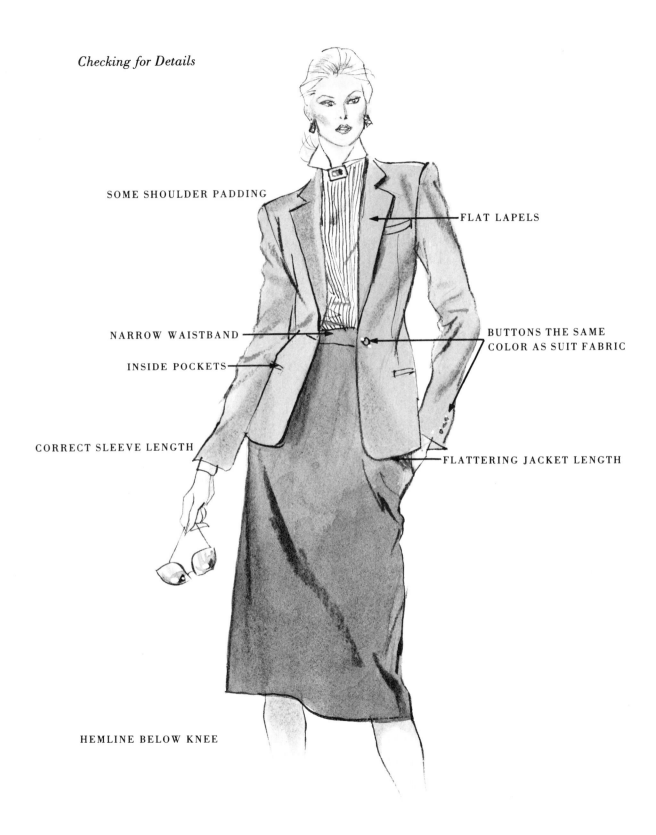

Checking for Details

SOME SHOULDER PADDING

FLAT LAPELS

NARROW WAISTBAND

BUTTONS THE SAME
COLOR AS SUIT FABRIC

INSIDE POCKETS

CORRECT SLEEVE LENGTH

FLATTERING JACKET LENGTH

HEMLINE BELOW KNEE

CHECKING THE FIT

The shoulders are the most important part of the jacket fit and are nearly impossible to alter. On most women, the shoulder seam should be about one quarter inch in from the edge of the shoulder. However, if a woman has narrow shoulders or sloped shoulders, the seam should rest directly on the edge of the shoulder. Armholes should not fit snugly. Being comfortable is tantamount to being well-dressed. Some padding in the shoulders will give an uplifted, attractive line. But extremely heavily padded shoulders are either very fashionable, very matronly, or too athletic-looking.

The collar and the lapel of the jacket should lie flat and not bulge. In more expensive suits, this area will be hand-stitched. In less expensive suits it will be machine done and probably glued. Watch out for an extremely stiff interfacing, because it may be a poor attempt to give substance to a limp fabric. It is a mark of a cheap suit.

The jacket length on a woman should stop at the most flattering place, which may be the waist, the hipbone, the top of the leg, or the thigh. For a man's suit there is one defined length to all jackets, but women should choose the length that is most flattering to their particular figure and stay with it.

The sleeves of the jacket should hit the wristbone. This allows for a blouse to show (although this is purely an individual preference) without making the jacket too long and dowdy-looking. Another way to measure is to bend the hand perpendicular to the arm. The edge of the jacket should just graze the hand.

The suit lining should be of good quality so it will not shrink or stretch out of shape. In contrast to the half lining of most men's jackets, almost all quality women's jackets are fully lined. The lining should match the fabric exactly and never hang below the bottom of the jacket. This is especially important to check after dry cleaning.

The waistband of the skirt should be rather narrow for the best look: no more than one and a half inches. The band should also be large enough so that it doesn't bind or roll. A too-tight waist will give a "spare tire" look, no matter how slender you are.

The skirt lining should be the same material as the jacket lining. It needs to be generous enough so that it will not bind but will move with the skirt.

Always sit down in a skirt before you buy it. When you sit, your rib cage expands. This can change the way a suit fits by making the buttons pull, the back wrinkle, or the waistband roll. You should also walk, move about, and pantomime any activity you regularly perform at work.

Remember that most of the time you will be viewed from the side or the back, rather than head-on. So take the time to check out all the angles in a three-way mirror.

IT'S A CONSTANT

Classically styled suits are an investment in your business future. The tailoring and the detailing will remain constant and travel with you from year to year with no confusion. A classic suit in your closet is like an Oriental rug on your living-room floor; it will outlast all the fads and fancies that come and go. It will endure, and most important, it will always look right.

□ 14 □

THE NEXT STEP: DRESSES, BLOUSES, AND SWEATERS

DRESSES FOR COMFORT

No other item of clothing in a woman's closet is likely to be as comfortable and attractive as a dress, nor does any other item offer such a prime chance to display a little individuality. A carefully-chosen dress can go to the office all by itself or it can be worn under a blazer or suit jacket for a look that has a little more clout.

A dress doesn't actually have to be a one-piece garment. A two-piece style makes it easier to get a good fit, top to bottom, and often the two pieces can each be worn with other items in your wardrobe. Generally, two-piece dresses look best on tall or slender women. Because of the extra fabric that may "blouse" out a bit around the waist, a two-piece dress will not flatter a woman with extra weight around the middle.

If you are planning to wear a dress with a jacket you already have in your wardrobe, bring it with you to the store or make sure you can return the dress if you get home only to find that the ensemble doesn't work. It is

163

particularly important that the collar of the dress and the collar of the jacket are in proportion.

The best-fitting dresses are those that have a definite waistline, in the form of sewn-in elastic or a waistband or a seam joining the top to the bottom. If a dress is cut with no waist, and depends on a matching fabric belt to supply the waistline, the result may be an unflattering shape. What usually happens is that the belt shifts around and either pulls the dress fabric or allows it to balloon out unattractively. This will have the effect of adding weight where you probably don't need or want it.

Most dresses, in fact, will look better if you throw away the fabric belt that comes with them and substitute a good-quality leather belt with an attractive buckle.

COLOR AND PATTERNS

You needn't be as concerned about sticking strictly to the basic women's business colors when you are buying dresses. Accent colors like cherry red, sapphire blue and even emerald green can be worn successfully in business as long as the tailoring is conservative. A dress can also be toned down, if the industry requires it, with the addition of a basic color jacket, like black or gray.

Too much unrelieved pastel color is not a good choice; but a pastel background, like yellow, with a dark accent color that is picked up in a jacket works well. Don't be afraid to use brighter colors, foulard or geometric prints, discreet stripes, or sophisticated abstract prints in very small patterns. Avoid oversize or splashy floral prints and large sporty-looking plaids.

FABRICS

Soft materials that skim but don't cling to the body are a better choice for dresses than thick, heavy fabrics. Avoid light, flimsy dresses that look too fragile to go to work in. Silk or silk blends or some of the exceptionally good silk lookalikes are perfect year-round. Heavier fabrics, like cotton and cotton blends, depending on their color, can be worn almost year-round. Linen-look blends are crisp and nice-looking for spring and summer months.

Again, the idea of appropriateness comes into play. A flowing material like chiffon, georgette, or voile is inappropriate for business wear and best used for "party" clothes. Denim, on the other hand, looks too sporty for the office.

Although expensive knit dresses and ensembles are quite sophisticated and show little wrinkling, they tend to be too country-club-looking for most women to wear successfully in business. The notable exception is the mature, exceptionally confident woman. She alone can carry off this look. But in general, this style is best left to the Nancy Reagans.

STYLING

Generally, one-piece dresses are very flattering to all figure types. Sometimes they are the only attractive option for a heavy woman.

Dresses come in two basic styles; the shirtwaist with a defined waist and the chemise without a defined waist. Every dress is a variation of one of these styles. For example, the double-breasted coat dress without a belt is a chemise, while the two-piece foulard print with a wide belt is a shirtwaist.

Interesting and appropriate details include:
- A white collar on a contrasting color
- Pintucking on the collar or down the front
- An asymmetrical closing
- Covered fabric buttons
- A versatile scarf attached to the neckline, tied in front or back

Dress skirts can be dirndl, gathered at the waist, pleated, or wraparound style. For wraparounds, make sure there is enough fabric to wrap

Shirtwaist

Chemise

comfortably around you and that it will withstand a sudden gust of wind.

When you are mixing dresses and jackets, the fabrics must complement each other as well as the styles. A tweed jacket won't look right with a thin cotton dress, and a linen blazer won't work over a wool flannel dress. But a tweed jacket over a wool dress does work, as does the linen blazer over a cotton dress.

Dresses, especially two-piece dresses, allow for the maximum amount of versatility and coordination within a wardrobe. For example, one two-piece dress in a small foulard print, with a solid suit and a separate jacket in a contrasting color or fabric, provides many options.

The versatility of two-piece dresses

BLOUSES: YOUR MOST VERSATILE ACCESSORY

Blouses can actually be considered accessories. A good suit or skirt and blazer combination will get you off to a good start, but it is the blouse that will finish off the outfit and stamp it as yours, by adding color, individuality, and style. One of the best reasons for selecting conservative suit colors and styles is to allow yourself to show a little pizzazz in choosing blouses.

Certainly the most versatile blouses are those in solid colors; but every working woman's wardrobe should include some patterned blouses in prints or stripes. These will really add some professional flair.

Look for nicely executed details on a blouse; these too, can spice up your suit looks. Long sleeves give the most professional look and this style can be worn year-round. For summer wear, a sleeveless shell is great, but it requires that you keep your jacket on all the time. Totally bare arms are never appropriate. A three-quarter-length sleeve or even a short-sleeve blouse can be worn for business, except for very conservative industries.

Some blouse details to look for:

- Covered fabric buttons will add richness.
- Slightly padded shoulders help a blouse keep its shape.
- Good-quality stitching enhances the look.
- Extra buttons included in a separate little envelope are a nice touch, and a lifesaver if you lose a blouse button.
- A placket concealing the top button or all the buttons is a very elegant detail.
- Narrow rows of vertical pintucking add interest and sophistication.
- Shoulders can be either flat or gathered; the flat look is a more conservative look; gathers are a bit more fashionable.

Bust darts should be avoided; they cheapen the look of the blouse and often mean inferior workmanship. Any shaping should be accomplished in the design and cutting.

Pay particular attention to the care that is going to be needed. Unlike a suit, a blouse will require frequent cleaning or laundering. Are you willing to invest the time and money to have a silk blouse professionally cleaned after every wearing or every other wearing? If not, better pass on that and buy a good silk lookalike in one-hundred-percent polyester that is easily laundered. If you hate to iron, forget about one-hundred-percent cotton.

BLOUSE STYLES

The most common is the *front tie bow;* it adds softness and femininity and is almost universally flattering. It is easy to wear and looks very good with a suit. The scarf should be attached to the blouse in the back so it will stay in place.

A *side tie* or an *asymmetrical closing* on the blouse is a very flattering, fashionable, and professional look.

A *V-neck* is a good neckline, so long as it is not too bare and doesn't reveal too much collarbone or any cleavage. Most often it requires some jewelry—possibly a string of pearls—to fill in the space. It is a good idea to try on a V-neck with any jackets you plan to wear, especially if the jacket has no lapel.

A *collarless* blouse can, by its very simplicity, be a nice complement for a suit. It will require some jewelry.

The softness of the *cowl neck* makes it a great choice, especially for an older woman who wants some concealment. Make sure the style is modified so there is no great excess of material.

The *mandarin or stand-up collar* is a very flattering look, especially with a collarless jacket. It can be complemented by a thin oblong scarf wrapped around the neck and tied in front for added color or detail.

The *button-down collar* is crisp and efficient-looking, but it is a very conservative look. Wear it sparingly. It is usually found in a cotton broad-cloth or oxford cloth. White and blue are the safest color choices, but selecting this style in other colors, or in a stripe, will soften the look.

The *boat neck* is a very attractive neckline that looks good under most suit jacket styles. Remember that bra straps may show if the cut is wide, so you need to select one with a smaller opening.

A *solid white collar* with contrasting bodice and sleeves in a solid or a small print provides a nice look. It is sometimes worn with a neatly tied scarf or bow.

An *ascot* is more formal and quite elegant. It's a good neckline to accompany a lapelled jacket. An antique stickpin in the ascot is a nice touch.

BLOUSE FABRICS

Most of the blouses sold today are made of one-hundred-percent polyester. The good man-made fibers are very hard to distinguish from real silk. They look and feel like silk, wear well, resist perspiration stains, and can be laundered easily.

Silk, of course, is not colorfast, and generally requires dry cleaning. If you perspire while wearing a silk blouse, the blouse color may bleed into the suit jacket, and any damage can be considered permanent; it is actually dyed in. Usually a silk blouse will show perspiration stains after a half dozen wearings.

Wool blends are not too commonly used as blouse fabrics, but they can add softness to a winter ensemble, and they are unbeatable for richness and longevity.

Cotton blends are good choices for more conservative blouses, with oxford cloth the most common. The blend is usually a mixture of cotton and polyester. Such a mixture will take a light starching and be more comfortable than the silk look-alike in hot weather. Cotton gabardine has a harder finish, and is a heavier material.

Linen blend blouses can sometimes double as loose jackets, but they are limited to warm-weather wear. Even in blends the fibers often break, causing permanent wrinkling. Linen is not colorfast.

Fabrics such as chiffon or brocade are too dressy for office wear. Denim and cotton knits are too sporty. All-rayon will wrinkle too easily.

Blouses must complement your jacket lapel

SWEATERS: AN APPROPRIATE ALTERNATIVE

Carefully selected, sweaters will perk up a woman's business wardrobe. The best ones are all-silk, all-cotton, or blends with these fibers in them. Business sweaters should be very closely knit but not tightly fitted.

Solid-colored, collarless sweaters are the best choices, because they accessorize well with jewelry, scarves, or blouses and they look especially good under tailored jackets. Textural variations are also attractive. Subtle weaves and patterns can be sophisticated when paired with a suit.

Avoid bulky, hand-knitted sweaters and fluffy angoras, which are appropriate only for sporty occasions. Any sweater that you wear to work should be completely opaque and not reveal the outline of your undergarments.

Remember your look will become more casual with a sweater than a blouse. But it offers a good alternative to blouses and it is appropriate dressing for many industries.

□ 15 □

THE FINE TUNING: WOMEN'S ACCESSORIES

In a business woman's wardrobe, accessories are the icing on the cake. They stamp a professional with a very personal style and are always worth special attention.

SHOES

Stick to real leather in basic colors—black, navy, dark brown, taupe, burgundy. The dark colors will complement your basic colored suits and your brighter-colored dresses, and the leather will assure you of a comfortable fit. If you are going to splurge on any item in your wardrobe, it should probably be your shoes, for reasons of both comfort and beauty. If your feet hurt, your face will show it.

Avoid white, pastel, or fashion-colored shoes, like purple, red, or turquoise; these colors will draw too much attention to your feet. White is really only appropriate for casual looks, worn with a white skirt or white pants. Your shoe color should generally be darker than the color of your hemline.

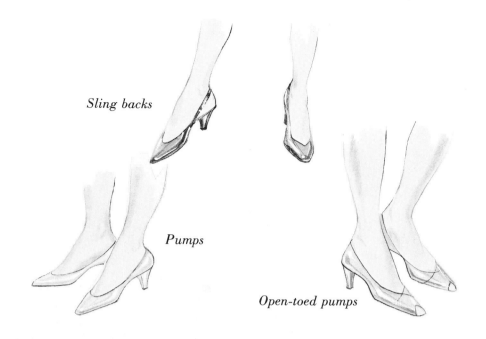

Sling backs

Pumps

Open-toed pumps

Stay with medium heels, at least two inches in height. They will flatter your leg because your muscle becomes elongated as you wear heels, making your calf slimmer. Absolutely flat heels will make you appear to be standing in a hole. Even if you are tall, a moderate heel will give you a more graceful walk that will be a better complement to your business attire. Extremely high heels will make you look top-heavy and cause you to pitch forward as you walk.

The most versatile style is the pump, with a closed toe and closed heel. This works year-round, with suits, dresses, and skirts and blazers. The sling back is also a good choice, if you can wear it gracefully and if you give proper attention to your heels so they are not ragged and chapped-looking. A sling back can be worn practically year-round (with the exception of very cold or snowy weather, when it would look too light), but it is especially attractive in spring and summer months.

A closed heel and slightly open toe is a very appropriate business shoe with a little more flair.

Strappy sandals are inappropriate for office wear; they are an off-the-job look that is too casual for most business outfits. Too much foot shows and sandals often are too sexy.

Not long ago I got on the elevator in a downtown office building in Atlanta with a young woman who was perfectly turned out from head to ankles: a well-cut black suit, white pintucked blouse with a stunning black and red silk scarf. Her hair and makeup were well done. The problem started at her ankles. She was wearing bright red sandals, with four-inch heels and ankle straps, and they truly detracted from her total look. An observer tended to focus on her sandals and nothing else. The style was too frivolous, the color too startling on her feet. The height of the heel made her walk very graceless.

Certainly shoes with interesting detailing—a small cut-out on the side or across the vamp—are very acceptable. But these details will limit you in what you can wear with the shoes. A better alternative is to purchase leather clip-on rosettes and bows to add to the vamp of your shoes. They will change the look from office to evening.

You should have at least three pairs of good-quality leather shoes that you alternate, since even the most comfortable shoes need to rest and reshape themselves, preferably with the assistance of shoetrees. Rotation also increases their lifespan. Black is always a good first choice, with burgundy, taupe, or navy as versatile colors for additional pairs.

Don't match your shoes exactly to your purse; they can match in color or texture, but not both. It's too contrived.

HOSIERY

Neutral-colored hosiery is the best look. Choose a color just a little darker than your skin tone, in a size that gives you room to move but does not "bag" at the ankles. Avoid any hosiery that has an orange cast: Black women should avoid hosiery with an ashy color.

For conservative businesses, neutral colors are really the only choice. But if your industry is more directed toward fashion and creativity, you might tone your hosiery to your skirt hem—but stay with sheer, not opaque, hose.

Don't ever be tempted to go bare-legged to the office, no matter how tanned and shapely your legs or how hot and sticky the weather. That is an extremely unprofessional look. The materials of your suits and most of your dresses will "clash" with your bare legs; your feet will swell and stick to the insides of your shoes and the total look will be a most unattractive one.

You should keep an extra pair of panty hose in your desk drawer and one in your purse or briefcase: Runs and holes are unattractive. Make an inspection of your hose—front and back—a standard part of your detail check. When you buy a new pair of shoes, check the insides carefully for rough spots or threads that can snag hose.

I do not recommend paying a lot of money for hosiery. Obviously a pair of forty-nine-cent panty hose is not going to wear well; but I've worn drugstore hose and designer hose, and I really can't tell the difference. Buy good quality hose, but don't pay $8.50 a pair. Save your money for something else.

SCARVES

Too many women underestimate the versatility of a good silk scarf or pocket square in pulling together an outfit or giving a "lift" to an aging ensemble.

It's nice to pick up a color from a print or striped blouse and wear the color as a solid pocket handkerchief in the breast pocket. Or, if you are wearing a solid color suit and blouse, you can choose a patterned scarf, using the blouse and suit color, and then add another accent color, to sharpen your look. For this reason, a breast pocket is a nice detail to look for when you are buying a jacket or blazer.

Silk is really the only appropriate fabric for a scarf; it will tie into a smaller knot and hold its shape much better than a scarf that is made of polyester. Never let too much of the scarf puff out, since you are after only a hint of color.

The versatility of an oblong scarf

KNOTTED IN FRONT

SECURED ASYMMETRICALLY

TIED IN THE BACK

Usually a scarf worn around the neck will replace any neckline jewelry. The oblong is the most versatile shape. Tie it in front or on the side, or give yourself a collar of color and tie it in the back.

JEWELRY

There is no substitute for *real* jewelry. Gold, silver, or pearl earrings, a gold or silver bracelet, an interesting lapel pin, an attractive and serviceable watch are all wise additions to a business wardrobe.

If the real thing is out of your reach, or you simply travel a lot and don't want to risk losing your gems, good-quality costume jewelry can be a boon to your wardrobe. The idea of costume jewelry originated with Coco Chanel, who was always losing her "real" pieces at work. Costume jewelry is generally slightly oversized—larger pearls for earrings, larger designs for "gold" earrings and bracelets. Let your good taste be your guide. Avoid fake stones that attempt to emulate precious gems like diamonds, emeralds, or rubies; but do use semiprecious stones or other substances—like tortoise or onyx. Just keep the proportion in mind. You don't want anything that dangles, clanks, or jingles. Good jewelry should be seen and not heard.

Costume earrings are generally larger sized than fourteen-carat gold. However, if you wear glasses, keep earrings smaller. You don't want to look like a tinseled Christmas tree. Avoid dangly earrings or hoops. Button earrings, in all shapes, are the best. If you wear earrings regularly, you should consider having your ears pierced: This style is more comfortable and more attractive and you are much less likely to lose an earring.

An authentic cameo—or a good imitation—looks very classy worn at the throat, particularly with a dark-colored suit. A square, woven gold pin is another versatile jewelry piece.

Rings should generally be limited to one on each hand, unless you have a matched wedding and engagement set that fits neatly together. Sparkling stones are fine, but avoid the oversized "dinner rings." No plastic rings, of course, and no pinky rings.

When you are choosing a watch, buy the best you can afford. Begin by looking at the costliest lines, then go back to your price range and select a model that incorporates as many of the design features of the more expensive ones as possible. The classic tank or Cartier styles are the most suitable: yellow or white gold with a black band is the most versatile choice. Stay away from expandable bands, unless you are investing in a Rolex, and avoid diamonds or other precious stones on the face of the watch. In general, it's better to put your jewelry money into jewelry, and keep your watch purchase separate.

A simple string of pearls—real, if you can afford them, or a good quality imitation—adds a note of elegance to a business outfit. Avoid anything that looks too obviously fake—like deep-red or blue-colored pearls. The classic off-white or pink shades are the best.

BELTS

Two or three leather or skin belts in a woman's wardrobe can "uplift" many of her ensembles. Most belts that come with ready-made dresses are simply cardboard covered with fabric and deserve to be discarded and replaced with a good-quality leather or suede belt. Black is the most versatile choice; but don't be afraid to try something interesting, like a black and burgundy snakeskin combination. Belting your clothes will give your outfit a finished look—even a classic suit skirt can benefit from belting. Just remember to leave the belt loose enough so that the waistband isn't constantly slipping out from under the belt. Even on a larger woman a definite waistline will be flattering and slimming. For versatility, choose a style that is one half to three quarters of an inch wide; wide belts are for women with small waists and no "spare tire."

Many shops are now offering "investment" belt buckles in gold or silver ranging in price from fifty dollars to two hundred dollars. They come with strips of soft leather that can be interchanged. This is often exactly what a mediocre outfit needs—a little pizzazz.

RAINCOATS AND TOPCOATS

Choose a classically styled raincoat, preferably in British tan. Because of the good-quality treatment given the fabric to make it water repellent, it will also resist soiling fairly well. The classic trenchcoat style is hard to beat. It has been correct for as long as anyone can remember and will no doubt continue to be. Women do have other color options—black or navy—that give a more fashionable but still very businesslike look.

Many women like the versatility of a raincoat with a zip-in lining. It can be a real boon for traveling, and in some temperate climates it may actually take the place of a winter coat. Do make sure you try the coat on with the lining in and out. If you are short or heavy, you will have to select your style carefully so that the lining doesn't add too much bulk. Most belted raincoats are actually worn tied rather than buckled—probably because it is faster to tie and untie rather than buckle and unbuckle. A raglan sleeve is the best style.

Make sure your raincoat is long enough to cover all your business skirts and dresses—another reason for adopting a permanent hemline in all your garments. Avoid plastic see-through coats, which look and often smell horrible.

A heavy winter coat should be one-hundred-percent wool for maximum warmth. Choose a basic color—like black, navy, brown, burgundy, gray, or tan. You don't want a stand-out color or large pattern, particularly something in a bright plaid that looks like a horse blanket. I also would not suggest a fur collar. A tweed is a good choice for daytime, but will not be as versatile as a solid color, which can be worn in the evening.

Cashmere is a very luxurious fabric, quite comfortable and usually a better business investment than a fur. Camel's hair is also a good choice for durability.

Both the polo wrap style and the full-length double-breasted style are good, classic selections.

A fur coat is acceptable for business only when it is needed for warmth. If your climate justifies the purchase of a fur coat, and your wallet can support it, stick to a classic styling because you will want to keep this investment a very long time. The stroller length and full length are the best buys because of their versatility. They can be worn with a business suit, a pair of jeans, or an evening dress. Stay away from leather inserts and "fun" furs like rabbit. They do not represent good value for your money. Fox, beaver, and raccoon are good choices, with lynx and coyote reserved for more glamorous industries. But mink will always be the most classic and conservative of furs and probably the best value for business wear.

GLOVES AND MUFFLERS

When the temperature drops, you'll be glad to have a pair of sleek leather gloves in a dark color that works well with your winter coat— probably a black or dark brown. Fur lining will ensure that your fingers stay warm. The gloves should be long enough so that no skin shows between the top of the glove and the edge of the coat sleeve. Knitted gloves are too informal for professional wear.

A soft woolen scarf or muffler will help keep out the chill while helping keep your collar free of makeup. Choose a dark solid or very subdued stripe or plaid in a soft, warm fabric. An acrylic will not provide much warmth—stick with one-hundred-percent wool, even cashmere, if you can manage it.

HATS

Unless they are needed for protection against snow or rain, hats are inappropriate for business women. They make too strong a fashion statement and are best saved for a social occasion.

However, in cold weather, warm hats are a necessity because a great deal of body heat is lost from the head. Select one that will do the minimum amount of damage to your hair style.

FOUL-WEATHER GEAR

If you live in snow country, you will have to be prepared for bad weather. Your black leather pumps aren't going to afford much protection if there is eight inches of snow on the ground. Choose a pair of practical, lined and waterproof snow boots, to keep you warm and dry. If you buy leather boots, be certain to weatherproof them with a spray for protection from the water and salt.

Wear your boots to and from work and carry your office shoes in your briefcase or a tote bag—or keep your black pumps at the office. Don't wear boots at the office all day because they will make your feet swell and they are also one of the causes of foot odor.

Hard-sided briefcase

Soft-sided briefcase

An excellent handbag for business

PURSES AND BRIEFCASES

If you carry a purse in lieu of a briefcase, make sure it is leather, in a dark color—black, brown, navy, and particularly burgundy are excellent choices. Scale it to your size and height.

Don't try to substitute a purse for a briefcase. However, carrying both a purse and a briefcase will make you look positively loaded down. It's one or the other.

Choose a sturdy, attractive briefcase—leather if you can afford it, or an excellent imitation leather. Burgundy is the most popular choice, followed by brown and black. Don't dilute the effect of a briefcase by choosing a light shade. Both a soft-sided and a hard-sided briefcase are appropriate choices for a business woman. Select the one that best reflects your style and your business. (For information on buying briefcases, see Chapter 11.) A leather notepad can often substitute for a briefcase.

Choose the smallest-size purse you can and don't stuff it unmercifully, because it will add a clumsy look to your appearance. It will also shorten the life of your handbag. If you need a really large purse, you will do better with a briefcase. Also be aware that others will see the contents of your purse when you open it; so don't fill your bag with wadded tissues.

Your wallet, which should be easily accessible, works best in a dark color, especially burgundy. It, too, should not be crammed with snapshots, credit cards, or even money. Carry only what you need.

□ 16 □

TAKING IT FROM THE TOP: WOMEN'S HAIR CARE

Your so-called crowning glory can be either a blessing or a curse. There is probably no single component of a woman's appearance that is as potent as her hair—certainly none that has a greater impact on how she feels. If your hair looks good, you can face the world. If there is something wrong with it, nothing else seems to go right, whether you are six or sixty.

In the business world, a fashionable hair style is one that is neat and appropriate—nothing extreme or overdone. Your hair should be something you spend no more than thirty minutes on in the morning, retouch at noon, and happily forget the rest of the day. If your hair style requires constant fussing, arranging, or spraying, it is inappropriate for the office.

The hair you wear to work should always be yours—no wigs, please. Regardless of the cost, wigs look like wigs. Cheap ones look like cheap ones, and expensive ones look only slightly better. Real hair moves; wigs do not. Real hair has a luster; wigs have a chemical sheen. Any hair style will look better than any wig. The only exception would be for a woman afflicted with a severe loss of hair.

The hairdo you select for your professional image should be flattering and easy to keep. This doesn't mean you should wear the same style year after year. Certainly all of us need our hairdo updated at least once a year.

One professional woman realized a change was in order when she saw a picture of herself in her college yearbook taken thirteen years earlier, and realized she was wearing essentially the same hair style. She changed her hair and felt and looked much more contemporary.

The other side of the coin is that no serious professional woman wants to be a slave to every weird hair idea her stylist brings back from the latest hairdressers' convention.

The exact length of your hair is pretty much a matter of individual taste, as long as you avoid inappropriate extremes. Very long, flowing, down-to-the-waist hair can be alluring and quite effective—in perfume ads or on entertainers. But it doesn't work in the office. That is not the place to try to look alluring, if you are serious about your career. Very long hair has too much of an Alice-in-Wonderland quality to make it effective in the business world, where the sex goddess and the little girl are truly out of place. And long hair that is scraggly and thin, stringing down your back, simply looks déclassé and cheap. Generally, anything past shoulder-length is too long, unless it is worn up all the time.

But don't go to the other extreme and opt for the sensible, no-care, no-style "do" in the hope it will look efficient, as though it is worn by someone with more important things to consider than hair. At best, it will look dowdy and give you the appearance of being unconcerned with details, insensitive to the way you appear to others, careless of your company's image. At worst, it will look "butch" and mannish unless you have an extremely feminine face.

When you are making a decision about your hair style, consider first your time constraints and the natural limitations of your hair. If your hair is thin and fine, don't waste your time trying to cultivate a thick curly mane. Try a short, feathery style that will soften your features and make the best of your hair and its texture. If your hair is thick and coarse, don't force a sleek close-to-the head bob. Longtime *Vogue* editor Diana Vreeland has described beauty simply as consistency. Having great-looking hair only for two hours in the morning doesn't lend itself to a consistent appearance.

Realistically, the less trouble every morning, the more likely you are to have a hair style that looks consistently good. Shorter hair is generally easier to maintain on a daily basis.

SHAMPOOING

Wash your hair as often as needed. Despite the persistent myth, daily shampooing does not make your hair fall out. Nor does waiting an extra day to wash your hair provide it with a natural oil treatment, as many women believe. It does provide a natural bacteria treatment, perhaps, but that is hardly beneficial.

Certainly hair can be damaged, but the damage is likely to result from thermal processes, like overuse of hot rollers and hot blow-dryers, or inept chemical processes such as a bad permanent. One hundred strokes a day of brushing will also damage your hair.

A very common form of damage is split ends. The only permanent way to handle this problem is to cut them off; no product can grow them back together, although some products will temporarily heal them between shampoos. Often split ends can be lessened simply by the regular use of end papers when you use hot rollers.

The best shampoos are the ones that need very little manipulation to create lather. The product should do the cleaning, not you. Hair is in its weakest state when wet, so one lathering should be the limit. And always use a conditioner after each shampoo.

Switch shampoos occasionally. Try sample sizes. Your hair can experience a "waxy build-up," so do change formulas when your present shampoo doesn't seem to be cleaning. Be leery of bargain-basement shampoos. They are often so diluted that you are actually getting less shampoo than with regularly priced products.

CONDITIONERS

Conditioners are actually very effective Band-Aids for the hair. They provide important protection from shampoo to shampoo and make your hair much easier to handle when it is wet. They will also give your hair some shine and combat static electricity.

A conditioner will separate the individual hair strands and make combing easier. All conditioners will work even better with heat. Wrapping a hot, moist towel around your head while the conditioner is still on or sitting under a dryer for five minutes with a conditioning product opens up the cuticle of each hair shaft and allows better penetration of the product.

Unless you have particularly thick hair, avoid creme rinses. They are too waxy. An easy way to condition flyaway hair in the wintertime is to run a sheet of fabric softener lightly over your hair and hairbrush. It will remove the static.

SELECTING A STYLIST

Every woman has, at some time or other, had a bad hair experience—a cut that was too short or a perm that was left on too long. Sometimes the culprit is a well-meaning friend who insists she has a way with hair. Sometimes we ourselves are to blame. (Have you ever decided at midnight that you just had to give your hair a quick trim?) But the worst experiences are usually those we pay for—often handsomely—on the occasions when a professional hair stylist ignores our requests, misunderstands what we asked for or simply doesn't have the required skill.

To avoid these frustrations, learn to say "no" to amateur hairdressers and do recognize that people cannot cut their own hair. Then take the time to find a stylist who will listen to you and understand your limited time as a working woman.

One of the best and easiest ways to find a good stylist is to ask three colleagues with good haircuts for their suggestions. Choose one and make an initial appointment for a consultation before committing to any scissor or coloring work. There should be no charge for this but be sure to ask. Start observing clients as soon as you walk in to see whether the hairdresser turns out conservative and beautiful business cuts or trendy, rock-star looks.

Always have your hair analyzed when it is dry. Bring some photographs to give your stylist an idea of what you want, but recognize they will serve only as guidelines. Never tell a new stylist to do anything he or she pleases. It isn't fair to you or your stylist. Have some idea of what you want and remember to give your new stylist as much information as possible about how your hair responds to various treatments. Don't hesitate to ask the price of anything and everything that your stylist recommends. Know the cost of upkeep on any changes.

Once you have decided on a stylist, do give him or her a chance. A regular stylist who knows your hair can be more helpful than a different one every month.

COLOR

Sooner or later practically every business woman gets the urge to try something different in the way of color. In fact sixty-five percent of the female population is using some type of hair color. It may be to cover premature gray hair or simply to lighten and brighten the hair.

A new hair color isn't likely, all by itself, to give you a new lease on life or ensure your promotion to vice-president. But it will certainly give your professional image a new dimension—if it is properly done. It can be an asset to your career.

Adding any color will improve the texture and condition of the hair. For fine hair that requires more body and volume, this is a real blessing. Blond will add the greatest amount of volume because each hair shaft is slightly "swollen" in the blonding process.

The desire to cover gray hair is one of the strongest motivations for professional women who try hair color, and it's a good motivation. In the business world, gray hair may look distinguished on men, but it usually looks mousy on women, because it is often a yellow-gray, rather than a silver-gray. But be wary of going darker than your natural color when covering the gray. You don't want the flat, shoe-polish look. Select a shade one step lighter than your natural color.

Before   (PHOTOS COURTESY OF CLAIROL)   *After*

There are several choices in hair coloring techniques:

- Rinses that last only until the next shampoo.
- Semipermanent color that lasts about five shampoos.
- Shampoo-in tints (which are permanent and require root touch-up).
- Double-process blonding for very dark hair that goes blond.
- Special effects—highlighting and frosting—that require much less maintenance because the results are more subtle.

The word "blond" brings to mind images of excitement, so most women who elect to do something opt for some shade of blond. But red tones have become increasingly popular for business women who have some naturally red highlights in their hair. Done properly, golden red can beautifully warm up a complexion and add polish to a professional appearance.

Recognize, if you apply the color yourself (which is the most popular method of coloring), that the model on the hair color box has had the color placed on her hair after all the natural color pigment was removed. That is why a very dark-haired woman can't use an ash-blond color and get ash-blond results. Always locate your natural hair color on the chart furnished by the manufacturer to determine what results you will get.

Black women should be aware that their curly hair shaft lends itself to more breakage and damage. The ethnic lines are manufactured to be extra-gentle and will probably yield better results than products manufactured for Caucasians.

Anyone using color should do a patch test to make certain that there is no allergic reaction to the product. Also do a strand test so you will be aware of the exact color you will obtain. When retouching, do only the roots at first and bring the color down on the rest of the hair for the last five minutes simply as a refresher.

PERMANENTS

Permanents were out of favor during the sixties, started a comeback in the seventies and are fully accepted today. For the business woman, they can provide the consistency that she requires in her daily appearance. The body obtained from a good perm will keep hair shaped and fresh all day.

Permanents are easier to give than they used to be. However, in the hands of those who don't know what they are doing, a permanent solution can be dangerous. Be certain that your volunteer hairdresser is proficient; otherwise have your hair curled professionally. One especially important part of the perming process is the rinsing. If all the solution is not rinsed out, the neutralizer will explode the ends and leave you with an extreme case of the frizzies.

Expect a perm to last six to twelve months, depending on the length of your hair. Never reperm over a perm unless you have exceptionally healthy hair. Generally it will cause breakage and frizzies. Never color and perm at the same time. It will damage your hair. Regularly use a deep conditioning formula for at least two weeks before having a permanent.

Body perms are very popular and produce a much softer curl. The same process is used for a regular perm except that the rods are fewer and larger.

For adding fullness and body, a quality permanent followed by color or highlighting several weeks later can turn limp hair into lovely hair.

17

PUTTING YOUR BEST FACE FORWARD: WOMEN'S SKIN CARE AND MAKEUP GUIDE

Face it—clean, healthy skin is the best thing you can "wear" on your face, for business or social occasions. You have probably already discovered that your skin "mirrors" your overall health and well-being. If you've been ill or not eating properly or staying up too late, the deficiencies are likely to show up in your skin.

Since we are viewed from the neck up more than seventy-five percent of the time, it makes sense to pay attention to the way our faces look. But before you even begin to think about makeup, make sure your skin is ready for it. All skin, of course, needs to be kept clean and free of dirt, bacteria, and old makeup; most skin will also benefit from a product that moisturizes and protects.

There are lots of skin care products on the market costing lots of money. Soaps alone are available in all sizes, shapes, colors, and fragrances, and the various creams, lotions, oils, gels, masks, toners, astringents, refiners, protectors, nourishers, and sunscreens available are too numerous to count.

Yet cost alone is no real indicator of quality.

In general, the cosmetics industry is pretty tightly regulated by the Food and Drug Administration, so even manufacturers of "dime-store" brands of cosmetics have to adhere to strict standards of purity, quality, and truth in labeling. Nor are the manufacturers permitted to make exaggerated claims on behalf of their products. If you cut through all the hoopla of cosmetics advertising and promotion with celebrity spokeswomen and glamorous long-haired females wearing filmy little nothings, you will notice that no skin care product manufacturer promises to alter the fundamental character of your skin. Their promises are in the more amorphous realm of a more beautiful you, inner glows, and new sparkles, and there's a good reason for that.

Basically, any product that could produce any substantial alteration in your skin would be a drug rather than a beauty aid, and the marketing and distribution of drugs is a whole different ball game, one that is even more tightly regulated than cosmetics distribution.

Thus, the cosmetics and beauty aid manufacturers must content themselves with making products that are pretty much like those made by their competitors, and seek their identity and niche in the market by finding a unique way to package or promote the product. Sometimes this is accomplished by a distinctive fragrance. Thus you are usually paying for the packaging and fragrance in a skin preparation rather than the basic ingredients of the product itself.

The chief ingredients in most cleansing creams and moisturizers are lanolin or jelly, both fairly inexpensive. It is possible to use other, costlier oils, but it is unlikely that they will perform any better than the old standards.

Occasionally a manufacturer and his advertising agency will go off on a tangent with a little razzle-dazzle about rare and exotic ingredients like queen bee jelly or coconut oil. None of those things is harmful—except, perhaps to your pocketbook—but they are sizzle, not steak. They can properly be regarded as ingredients that give products a pleasant fragrance or color or texture, the modern-day "snake oil," if you like.

In general, the almond-scented hand lotion that you buy in the grocery store is going to soothe your chapped hands as well as the status brand body cream you purchase in your favorite specialty store.

Buy the preparation that is "fragrance-coordinated" with your favorite perfume or bath powder, if you like the way it smells or looks, but do understand that you are not necessarily buying the best because you have paid the highest price.

SKIN TYPES

Each of the three types of skin—normal, oily, and dry—and combinations of these will benefit from a different kind of care.

Normal skin is nicely balanced, and usually relatively free of blemishes. Generally, it just needs to be kept clean, toned daily and protected with a thin coating of moisturizer. But it should never be neglected or taken for granted. Even skin that is normal in texture tends to dry out with the aging process, so it's wise to pay attention to potential trouble spots—around the eyes and at the corners of the mouth—before they show the first signs of lines or wrinkles.

Oily skin is characteristically shiny, with large, dilated pores; the surface never appears to be perfectly clean. It is more prone to acne and blemishes than other skin types, but does not wrinkle easily.

One of the most common mistakes made by women with oily skin is to overcleanse with harsh soaps that can destroy the skin's natural protective acid mantle, thereby creating a too-alkaline breeding ground for bacteria that will aggravate the skin's propensity for blemishing.

Thus, a slightly acidic soap is the best choice. Apply it with your fingers, a clean wash cloth (changed daily, since bacteria thrive in warm, wet terry cloth), or an abrasive sponge.

Washing should be followed by a deep pore cleanser or astringent, which should contain isopropyl alcohol. Alcohol used by itself is too drying, but it is effective when it is combined with other ingredients, such as sulfur, allantoin, resorcinol, or lanolin.

Powder can be a boon to a woman with oily skin, but it should be used sparingly and applied with a soft brush or a fresh cotton pad that is replaced daily, never with the original puff, which is a source of dirt and bacteria.

Even women whose skin is generally oily may have occasional dry patches. The answer is simply to treat each section of the face as it needs to be treated. Use a moisturizer only on the dry sections, to even out the texture of the skin. Women with oily skin should use eye cream, since there are no oil glands at all in the very thin skin that surrounds the eyes.

Dry skin plagues most women over the age of thirty and is a consequence of the normal aging process. Dry skin occurs when the skin loses moisture and natural oils. Simply adding oil to the surface of your skin will not plump out dry skin cells. For that, you need a combination of lubricants, emollients, and water.

The best source of this combination is a water-based product, rather than one that is oil-based. A greasy residue on your face is more likely to clog your pores and add to your complexion problems than to put new life in your skin.

A light-textured moisturizing cleanser is much better for dry skin than thick, greasy creams. Follow the cleanser with a mild toner. If the toner stings, simply wet a cotton pad before you apply the toner.

SOAPS AND CLEANSERS

Your skin, regardless of type, should be cleaned thoroughly twice a day; in the morning before you apply your makeup, and at night to remove the makeup and the day's accumulation of dirt. No matter how tired you are, you are not excused. As a cleaning agent, the soap and water combination is pretty hard to beat; many dermatologists consider it the most effective way to get your skin clean. A good soap should clean without irritation and without destroying the skin's naturally protective acid mantle. Cleansing creams, which contain water, oil, wax, and numerous other additives, including fragrance, are favored by many women with normal or dry skin.

Once your skin is clean, the next step is toning and exfoliating, or getting rid of impurities and dead skin cells. This should be done daily. Men accomplish this by their daily shaving, but women must make other arrangements. The toner, properly keyed to your skin type, should be applied with a flat cotton pad, rather than a cotton ball. This will use less cleanser and make the entire process more effective. Although there is no cosmetic on the market that will permanently reduce the size of the skin's pores, the toner will swell the skin around the pores and temporarily make them appear smaller.

The next step, for all but the oiliest skins, is moisturizing. The process gives the skin a thin, protective film and provides water to help plump out the skin cells. For this reason, it is water rather than oil or grease that should be the major ingredient in any moisturizer. All the other ingredients merely seal in the water; they don't provide any direct moisturizing benefit.

A good moisturizer will not only add water to the skin but will also keep the moisture from evaporating. Beneficial ingredients are lanolin, petrolatum, mineral and sesame oil, PABA, and paraffin. A moisturizer should never be greasy; instead it should be absorbed almost instantly into the skin.

The rate of absorption depends on the formula of the particular product. If the wax and oil have a high melting point, the cream will not feel greasy; rather, it will seem to have vanished from your skin (thus the old-fashioned term "vanishing cream"). But if the product has a consistency like vegetable shortening and a low melting point, like cold creams, then it will feel greasy.

The best time to moisturize the skin is right after a bath or shower, when the skin cells have had the opportunity to "drink" their fill and are receptive to a protective film. Lips should receive their share of moisturizer, since they contain no oil glands.

Cleansing and moisturizing creams may clean or protect, but they won't do much beyond that. Unfortunately, there is no brand of cream on the market that will stop the normal aging process or remove wrinkles. There are products that can minimize them, with a little camouflage or temporary smoothing out. Plastic surgery can help. But, basically, nothing can make forty-five-year-old skin look twenty-five.

ACNE

Although it is usually regarded as the plague of adolescence, acne can persist well into the twenties. Severe cases can cause blemishes and even scarring on the neck, shoulders, and back as well as on the face.

Unfortunately, there is no absolute cure for acne, but there are a number of things that can be done to minimize its effects. The best advice is to keep the skin clean: Wash it three times a day with a nonalkaline soap and follow up with an alcohol-based astringent. Products containing sulfur, allantoin, and benzoyl peroxide can be helpful. Makeup can help, too. Use a coverup product on the blemished areas, then a light foundation, carefully blended, over that, but do use a light hand. If you glop on the makeup, it will only serve to attract more attention to the blemishes you are trying to conceal. A well-balanced diet, light on sugar and greasy foods, is a good idea, too.

If your acne is severe, consult a dermatologist or seek the help of a professional skin care salon. Do remember, though, that salons are in business to make money, which they do by selling skin care products, cosmetics, and special services. The reputable salons will try to help you look and feel better by showing you products that can aid your particular problems. The less reputable ones will try to capitalize on your fears and insecurities and load you up with hundreds of dollars worth of expensive cosmetics that you may or may not need.

Although no one with a skin problem or acne ever quite believes this, it is true that the problem is much more obvious to you than to anyone else.

SUN AND SKIN CARE

If you're still baking your skin in the sun's ultraviolet rays every summer, probably nothing you read here or anywhere else is going to make you change your ways. It has been proven conclusively that frequent exposure to the ultraviolet tanning rays can promote skin cancer and will certainly result in leathery, coarse skin that will look older than its years.

For some reason, Americans can't seem to get over their infatuation with the false notion of "healthy" well-tanned bodies.

If you do spend a lot of time outdoors, particularly near the water, take some precautions—namely a sunscreen. There are several good brands on the market, and any one will work as long as it contains PABA, which can block the ultraviolet rays. Be sure to reapply every hour, since swimming or perspiration may wash it off, and be especially careful to use it on your face—around the eyes and mouth, for sure.

HYPO-ALLERGENIC COSMETICS

Hypo-allergenic cosmetics, free of ingredients that are known to be irritating to sensitive skin types, are great for women with skin allergies; but they can be beneficial to anyone who simply wants a gentle makeup, free of irritants.

There is a difference, however, between "natural" and hypo-allergenic cosmetics. Natural preparations may include almond oil, cocoa butter, or sesame-seed oil in lieu of synthetic ingredients, and many natural brands eschew preservatives.

Generally, preservatives are essential in cosmetics, because they help keep them free of bacteria. Without preservatives, mascara would probably have to be replaced every two weeks, since a mascara tube provides a fertile medium for bacteria that can cause eye irritation and infections.

For many years hypo-allergenic cosmetics were the cosmetics industry's poor relation: The colors available were often drab and unappealing, but the manufacturers have pretty much caught up with the rest of the business.

It is possible to develop allergies to a particular ingredient, fragrance, or chemical literally overnight, and it is equally possible to "grow out of" the same allergy, as your body chemistry changes.

A variety of foods, environmental pollution, even stress can all play a part in creating new allergies. If you find yourself with an unaccustomed skin problem, try switching your brand of cosmetics or perhaps try a hypoallergenic or fragrance-free line. Even a cosmetics brand that has been your faithful friend for several years can "turn" on you, if the formula is altered, or one ingredient is substituted for another. If the label of your brand says it "may contain" a particular ingredient, that is a tipoff that the formula of the product is subject to change from one batch to another.

MAKEUP

There's no such thing as a woman who doesn't look better with makeup. It conceals, smooths, and polishes, and it should be worn by every business woman every day. But your makeup should enhance your appearance, not stop traffic. Take the time to apply it carefully and blend it thoroughly.

FOUNDATIONS, COVER CREAMS, AND TONERS

Foundations are not intended to mask your face or give you an instant tan. Their purpose is to conceal blotches, discolorations, and imperfections and make the skin a proper background for the rest of your makeup. They should not be used in an attempt to change the color of your skin. A fair-skinned woman who tries to "tan" her face with dark makeup will look unnatural and aged.

Choose a foundation color that doesn't stray too far from your natural skin color. Otherwise, you will end up with a line of demarcation. The best place to test a foundation shade, not surprisingly, is where you will be wearing it—on your face, preferably at the jawline. Putting a dab of makeup on the back of your hand will simply tell you what the foundation looks like on the back of your hand. Unless your skin is extremely dry, you are better off with a water-based foundation than with one that is oil-based.

To apply, simply blend the foundation in downward strokes and short, feathery motions. Be especially careful to blend at the jawline, so you don't have a harsh line that shows where the makeup stops. Don't apply foundation on your neck or throat; all that will do for you is soil the collars of your garments.

If you need some spot concealment, use a special cover cream under your foundation. Choose a shade no more than one or two shades lighter than your skin tone. Use the cream on the circles under your eyes—we all have them, regardless of how much sleep we get—and on blemishes. The cream should not be greasy and heavy. Apply it lightly, and keep it away from the corners of your eyes, since that is where the first age lines appear and this will only serve to accentuate them.

If you have severe discoloration or a birthmark, investigate the Lydia O'Leary Covermark cosmetics line; it works miracles.

BLUSH AND POWDERS

Blushes add definition to the contours of your face and give you a bright, vivacious look. They are available in gel, cream, and powder form, in a great variety of colors.

Gels work best on very young skin, since they are water-based and won't aggravate skin problems. They provide a nice glowy transparent sheen and give the most natural look of all the blushes available. More mature skin, however, absorbs the color fairly rapidly and will benefit from a cream or powder form of blush.

Cream blushes are descendants of old-fashioned rouge. Cream blush moves well on the skin, provides good color and works nicely on dry or normal skin. Unfortunately, it is easy to make a mistake and use too much blush, so that you end up looking like a circus clown. Careful blending is the solution.

Powder is probably the most popular form of blush and the favorite of women with combination skin. It has good staying power. Properly applied, it can give an illusion of finely chiseled cheekbones that is not possible with cream or gel. But it is not recommended for the woman with dry skin, because it tends to collect in the fine lines on the cheeks and draws attention to them.

Burgundy-toned blush is the safest color, since it looks good on most women. Avoid bright red, orange, or the brick shades—or anything with a yellow tinge. Apply blush on the "apple" of your cheek, the part that is plumped out when you smile. Use your fingers for cream or gel and a clean, soft sable brush for the powder. Don't apply it too close to your nose or any lower than level with your earlobes.

Face powder can be helpful for normal or oily skin. Apply it after you put on a powder blush, but before you use a cream or gel. Choose a loose, translucent powder with no color, and apply it with a clean, soft sable brush—never a powder puff. Tap the powder gently into the brush, apply lightly to your face, then use a soft baby brush to soften all the lines. This will really set your makeup. Carry neutral-toned compressed powder with you for touchups.

EYE MAKEUP

Eyes are the natural focal point of the entire face. Using your eyes effectively to make eye contact will establish you as someone who is confident and direct. Eyes, for most women, are potentially their best feature, but they are often underplayed. It actually takes very little makeup to emphasize or dramatize the eyes, and the rewards are considerable. Women who wear glasses should pay particular attention to their makeup, so their eyes won't get lost, and they should use a heavier-than-normal application.

Begin with an eye shadow base over the eyelids; the shadow will last longer and will be less likely to settle in the creases. Used properly, eye shadow can highlight, emphasize, enlarge, or make eyes appear smaller; used improperly, it can spoil the effect of your entire makeup application.

Remember that the purpose of eye shadow is to make you look good, not to overwhelm. The best choice is a powdered shadow, applied with a sponge applicator, sable brush, or fresh Q-tip. Cream shadows do not last as long, and are more likely to crease.

Visually push back the brow bone by applying a dark shade of eye shadow on the crease and a lighter shade on the eyelid. Avoid glittery frosted shadows since the mat shades are much more flattering. Use a color that contrasts with your eye color. If you have *brown* eyes, try mauve, burgundy, or steel-blue shadow; for *blue* eyes, mauve, brown, and rose are good. For *green* eyes, steel blue, brown, or rose are good choices. Very *dark* eyes can use bronze, deep plum, or deep blues effectively. Don't try matching your shadow color to your eyes. The shadow shade will always overshadow your eye color.

Eyebrows determine the expression you wear on your face, so make sure your expression is the one you want the world to see. If your brows are arched too high, you will look permanently surprised; if they are tweezed to a fine, thin line, you will look grim. The best-looking brows are those that appear natural, but it is often necessary to give nature a helping hand and do a little judicious tweezing between the brows and underneath the brow line—never from the top.

Unless your brows are very thick and dark, you will probably need a little help filling in the brow line. For this, you are much better off using brush-on eyebrow color than an eyebrow pencil. Nothing will make you look like a refugee from the fifties more quickly than too much brow pencil. Choose a brow color several shades lighter than your hair color. Women with blond, white, or gray hair, though, should choose a color only slightly darker than their hair. Brush the color on using short, feathery strokes rather than one continuous line.

To line your eyes, use a soft crayon liner rather than a liquid liner. Simply take your crayon and draw a line at the base of the lashes, starting at the outer corner. Depending on the shape of your eye you will probably need to stop halfway rather than encircling the eye totally.

Always line the bottom lashes. For top lashes try a darker shadow applied next to the lash line for a softer look. Practice until you find the application that works best for you and your professional look.

Before you pick up your mascara, use an eyelash curler—but always on clean, dry lashes, to prevent breakage. Make sure the rubber grip is clean and free of cracks—and be careful to curl only the lashes, not your eyelid.

Mascara provides the finishing touch for the eyes. It is probably the single cosmetic that most women feel comfortable using. Regardless of your coloring, the best mascara colors are black or brown-black. Plain brown, by itself, is simply not dramatic enough. Apply mascara lightly and evenly, from the base of the lashes to the tip, on top and bottom lashes. Two or three thin coats will look better and last longer than one thick coat.

LIPSTICK

Lips are second only to the eyes in determining how you "look," yet many women regard lipstick as an afterthought—if they regard it at all. A surprisingly large number of women simply refuse to wear lipstick. Others put it on in the morning and don't bother with a reapplication for twenty-four hours.

Many women complain that lipstick simply doesn't stay on—and, to a certain extent, this is true. The Food and Drug Administration, some time ago, ordered cosmetics companies to stop using several red and blue dyes that were thought to be carcinogenic; those dyes that are now available simply lack the staying power of the old ones.

It is worth the effort, though, to keep your lipstick fresh; it adds an attractive bit of color and protects the lips. It also gives definition to the mouth area, which is where people often look when you are speaking.

Selecting the right lipstick shade is important. The color should flatter your teeth and work with your coloring and makeup, but it should not match your outfit exactly. A red-toned lipstick is a good choice for most skin types; it will make your skin and teeth look clean. Think in terms of a true cherry red. If the color is too garish, no one will see anything but your mouth.

If your makeup is fairly soft, stay with the pinks and corals. Burgundy-toned lipsticks complement most skin tones. Avoid pink lipsticks that have too much blue in them; they are not flattering. Most women are also well-advised to avoid yellowish or brownish tones in lipstick, since they make the skin look sallow and the teeth appear mottled.

If you use a lip liner, choose a color that is slightly darker than your lipstick shade. Outline your lips, then fill in with lipstick. Use your lipstick brush to blend the lipstick in with the liner, so you won't have a visible outline.

Keep a tube of lipstick and a small mirror in your attaché case and another in your desk drawer to permit quick, discreet touchups. It is not a good idea to apply lipstick in the middle of a business meeting or a sales call, or at your restaurant table. But it is worth the effort to maintain color on your lips.

18

THE FINAL TOUCHES: GROOMING DETAILS FOR MEN AND WOMEN

The fine-tuning that you do to your image represents time well-spent. Detail plays a crucial role in pulling together your overall professional look. It is the support system for the rest of your appearance.

YOUR PEARLY WHITES

Americans are the most teeth-conscious people in the world. Our high standard of dental care is the envy of people in other countries, although here it is something that we take for granted. Accordingly, we assume that everyone has good teeth and are surprised when we encounter someone who doesn't. The people you meet notice your teeth within the first sixty seconds of your encounter. Very crooked or discolored teeth look unhealthy and unprofessional. Straight, unstained teeth are a tremendous advantage.

A successful European businessman became quite self-conscious about his teeth when he moved to the United States; he made the decision to have them capped—something he never would have done had he chosen to remain in Europe, where teeth are not accorded such importance.

Although it was an expensive and time-consuming undertaking, capping his teeth has had positive personal and business results. His entire personality seemed to change for the better. He found himself smiling more because he was proud of his teeth and no longer self-conscious. Not surprisingly, he found that a lot of people smiled back.

Good dental care is essential for healthy and attractive teeth. This includes twice-daily brushing and daily flossing, which many dentists now say is even more important than brushing. The combination of brushing and flossing will remove food particles and plaque from between the teeth, to keep gums healthy and prevent bad breath.

When you are choosing a toothbrush, select one with soft bristles; the harder ones may harm your gums. Most business people keep an extra toothbrush, tube of toothpaste, and container of dental floss in their desk drawer. Brushing your teeth in a public restroom after lunch or before a meeting is not only acceptable but also very smart.

Beyond do-it-yourself care, you should always have your teeth professionally cleaned twice a year.

CROWNING OR ORTHODONTICS

If your teeth are extremely unattractive, capping may be the answer for you, as it was for the European businessman. This actually gives you a whole new set of teeth placed on your "real" ones. Done correctly, caps look very natural. Depending on whether it is a cosmetic procedure or one necessary to maintain your teeth, your firm's dental insurance may cover part of the cost. Often your dentist will let you work out a payment schedule for the remaining part. Otherwise, you might want to check into low-cost dental work provided by students, under supervision, at nearby schools of dentistry. Remember, though, the waiting list is usually long and the procedures themselves may take longer because of the students' slower work pace.

Just because you are out of junior high school, don't think you are too old for braces. Many adults are wearing braces to correct overbite problems or crooked teeth, often conditions that have plagued them since adolescence. When I started my company in 1979, I was wearing braces (for the second time, no less). There were times when it was difficult to smile at a prospective client and wait for his or her reaction to my mouth full of metal, but the final results were worth the effort.

In fact, braces today are so much improved that in many cases they are virtually unnoticeable. Often they can be attached to the back of the teeth or are made of a clear material that is very unobtrusive. Some problems can even be corrected by wearing a retainer at night.

Bleaching may be the solution for someone with discolored teeth. This procedure is well known among movie stars and television performers and is now filtering down to the general business population. A concentration of hydrogen peroxide plus an agent that allows for penetration is applied to several teeth at one time. The cost runs about ten dollars per tooth. Remember, though, that the natural tooth color is not pure white, but shades of yellow, so the bleaching procedure should be performed only on teeth that really need it. Call your local dental association for qualified dentists familiar with this procedure.

I can't overstate the importance of healthy, attractive teeth for business. Fortunately, today, nearly all problems can be corrected.

HANDS AND NAILS

Scarlett O'Hara was wrong on at least one count: people do notice your hands. Well-groomed hands and nicely manicured nails are part of any business person's total appearance. Every time you shake a hand, sign a document, or demonstrate a computer your hands are on display. If you're a nail-biter with ragged, bleeding cuticles, you appear to be tense, not in control of your situation. If your nails are chipped and broken, with traces of last week's polish, you look sloppy and inattentive to details. Like all other aspects of your appearance, your hands will work either for or against you.

For starters, hands should be scrupulously clean. If you tinker with cars or refinish furniture, either wear thin surgical gloves or push bar soap underneath the nails before starting a messy project. You don't want to wear even a trace of grease under or around your nails. Both men and women need twice-a-day hand cream applications in the cold weather. Chapped hands feel as bad as they look.

Everyone needs a weekly manicure; this means thorough cleaning underneath and around the nails, gentle scrubbing with a nail brush and pushing back the cuticle with an orange stick. Buffing is great for the nails. Women can maintain a high gloss and men a less shiny one.

The shape and size of your nail beds will give you an indication of whether or not you are likely to grow long nails. Some people simply can't. If your nail beds are very flat, then you are probably one of them. If the beds are gently rounded, then you will probably be able to grow nails with little trouble. Whatever their length, make certain that your nails are well-tended. They should all be approximately the same length. When a woman's hand is turned over with the palm up, at least an eighth of an inch of nail should be visible. Shorter than this and her fingers will look stubby. Extremely long nails belong on a lady of leisure, not a business woman.

Nail polish can definitely be a part of a professional woman's appearance, but only if it is not chipped or neglected. Shades should be in a range of soft roses and pinks—no oddball purples, blues, or anything with a yellowish cast. Stay away from too much irridescense or pearlization, which is not as professional looking as a mat cream formula and may even cause irritation. Lighter colors will wear better and make the nails seem longer. Darker shades will require more frequent touching up.

Unpolished, buffed nails, nicely shaped, are just as attractive as polished nails. And they require much less maintenance.

FRAGRANCE

Our reaction to any fragrance or scent is immediate, emotional, and often quite strong. We will love it or despise it.

Fragrance reaction can also be unconscious. When a coworker always reminds you of your childhood summers, it may be that her perfume contains the fragrances of flowers that grew each summer in your backyard. Another colleague's cologne may remind you of your first boyfriend.

But it can work the other way, too. If you happen to wear the same cologne that your boss's ex-spouse used to wear just before he or she withdrew all the money from their joint savings account, then your boss may dislike you, without even realizing why. If a client dislikes fragrances or is allergic to certain ones, then you will not endear yourself by overdoing your cologne application.

So the safest advice is to not wear any fragrance at all for business. Should that be totally out of the question for you, then go very light for daytime wear. Men should not wear concentrated colognes, only lighter colognes and aftershaves. Women should select a fragrance that is very light. Apply it sparingly. Remember, the fragrance may linger on your clothing, so you will be wearing more of it than you realize. Your own nose, accustomed to the scent, is not the most reliable judge of how much is too much.

If you've ever been on a crowded elevator in the morning, when Old Spice is at war with Hai Karate, which in turn is fighting Opium and Brut, then you are aware of how offensive fragrance can be.

The wise candidate will not wear fragrance on interviews. Neither will the smart salesperson wear fragrance when meeting new clients. You can never go wrong without fragrance, but you can make a big mistake by wearing it, despite what the cosmetics companies would like you to believe.

DEODORANTS

Even if you don't perspire heavily, you need a good underarm product that you apply daily. Since your body chemistry changes periodically, you may need to switch brands accordingly. A deodorant will stop the perspiration odor; an antiperspirant will help prevent the wetness.

Food with caffeine, like coffee and cola drinks, may increase the odor associated with perspiration. So will heavily spiced foods. Tense situations also produce strong odors. Both men and women can benefit by wearing underarm shields or pads when anticipating a difficult day.

Cleaning underneath your arms with an astringent, which kills bacteria, and then applying an underarm product will cut down on most of the odor. Removing the underarm hair either by shaving or close clipping is a quick way to eliminate a breeding ground for bacteria. Most women do shave underneath their arms and more and more men are clipping their hair for extra assurance.

Remember, normal perspiration is healthy; it is nature's way of cooling down your body. The problem arises when the odor is unpleasant or when the wetness is excessive. (See Chapter 5 on fabrics.)

□ 19 □
BODY LANGUAGE IN THE BUSINESS WORLD

What we say with our bodies—our eyes, hands, walk, eyebrows, and facial expressions—often comes out louder and clearer than the words and sentences we choose. It is much more difficult to "lie" with our body language than with our speech, probably because speech is largely an intellectual process and body language is often a reflexive or involuntary action. It can be controlled, but not many people bother to do so. Remember Captain Queeg in *The Caine Mutiny*, who destroyed his credibility on the witness stand while he nervously fingered two little ball bearings? Body language is a special combination of your physical characteristics, mannerisms, emotions, intellect, and nervous system.

Actually body language is the very first "language" we used the first year or so of our lives. Only gradually did we add speech. So it makes sense that our communication now involves a combination of verbal and nonverbal actions.

Although our body language remains an important means of communication, not many people give it the attention it deserves or use it as effectively as they could. Much of it is very nearly subconscious, yet it can be controlled or modified. Nail-biters and hair-twisters can learn to control their nervous mannerisms; people with a slumped-over, apologetic walk can learn to stand up straight.

In business, good body language is simply another weapon in your achievement arsenal, and an extremely effective one. An understanding of body language will make it easier for you to use it to send effective messages to those with whom you come in contact and it will also help you read other people's body language more accurately. You will be amazed at how much you can learn about them, including many things they might prefer that you not know.

The single most important tool in business is communication; it is no exaggeration to say that the effectiveness of our communications will determine the effectiveness of our business life. In communications, body language will work either for you or against you; you should resolve to make it an asset.

INVOLVING OTHERS

A comfortable entrance will start you off on the right foot in more ways than one. If you are walking into someone's office, you will have a period of about five seconds during which your "host" will be making an evalua-tion. Your entrance and the way you carry yourself can put him in a receptive frame of mind, so that he is willing to listen to what you have to say, or it can convince him to get rid of you as soon as possible.

Just as your entrance begins this involvement, a good, firm handshake takes it a step further. Eye contact continues and intensifies the involve-ment. Before he realizes what is happening, your host finds himself re-sponding to you—shaking your hand, returning your gaze, smiling back at you, offering you a chair, preparing himself for conversation. When that happens you are already ahead of the game. He or she is ready to listen.

The person in charge often issues directions through body language. If he or she remains standing, a subordinate will stand up. Once the boss is seated, a visitor to his office feels freer to sit.

Learning to receive and send body language effectively can make people comfortable with you, make them like you, and most important, make them want to do business with you.

WORDS VERSUS DEEDS

We are usually held more accountable for our words than for our body language. Yet when one contradicts the other, we tend to believe the body language more readily. "No, I don't mind if you smoke" is not very convincing if the person saying it is frowning, with eyebrows close-knit, as he moves away from you. "Yes, I'd love to work late tonight," no matter how loudly it is spoken, cannot be heard over the noise of a deep sigh, shrugging shoulders, and drooping head.

If someone professes to you that he is not angry, but does it with a red face, bulging neck veins, and bugged eyes, you are not at all sure he means what he says.

If a prospective buyer says, "That's very interesting," all the while yawning, drumming his fingers and looking around the room, don't count on making the sale.

On the other hand, two people can be having a heated discussion over a particular issue, but if their body language is still relatively comfortable, this indicates that the relationship—whether it is a personal or a professional one—is stable, despite the differences of opinion.

MAKING IT WORK FOR YOU

Body language can show acceptance of verbal communication. Nodding is a very effective way to show someone that you agree without actually saying so. Direct eye contact will indicate that you are interested in what is being said.

Contrast this with the feeling communicated by someone who does not make eye contact, but looks around the room or at his watch or fingernails, or someone who frowns or shakes hs head as he listens.

We are all subject to nervous gestures: We tap our fingers, jiggle our feet, or push up our glasses. Or we bite our nails, chew our lips, click our pens. All of these gestures are ways of reducing tension, letting off steam, and calming ourselves—in the same way a baby sucks her thumb or reaches for a favorite toy to stroke. And there is no reason to rid yourself of all of them: You don't want to turn yourself into an emotionless robot.

Certainly many of these gestures are an integral part of your being. Yet it is important to analyze the kinds of motions and gestures you make when you are tense and determine whether they are simply quirky personal habits (running your fingers through your hair, straightening your tie) or whether they are distracting traits that annoy, perhaps even anger other people (jangling car keys or pocket change, drumming your fingers loudly). Remember, these gestures may give away more information about your personality than you realize. Take a realistic view of yourself and how you project: Looking at yourself on videotape will be very self-revealing. You can discover both strengths and weaknesses.

DANGER ZONES

Guard against revealing more than you mean to. Watch out for these signs.

EYEBROWS

Eyebrows can often say as much about you as your eyes. Raised eyebrows indicate nervousness, surprise, or questioning. Brows knitted together in a frown register consternation, perplexity, sometimes indecision. Arched brows can communicate scorn and ridicule. Hair styles that conceal your brows deprive your colleagues of a chance to read the signals your brows are sending.

HANDS

It's very hard to "lie" with your hands. Shaking or fidgeting hands are dead giveaways that you are nervous or tense. Hands that play with pencils, fold and refold pieces of paper, or tap pens belong to very impatient or distracted individuals.

One of the most common manifestations of nervousness is the complaint that an individual doesn't know what to do with his or her hands. Men found a fairly simple solution a long time ago; they put their hands in their pockets, a gesture that immediately gives a more relaxed, more confident stance, and is particularly good when you are making an informal presentation—as long as you don't ruin the effect by playing with pocket change or jingling your keys.

More and more women are buying dresses and skirts that have side pockets so that they can have the advantage of the same comfortable zone.

FEET AND LEGS

A great deal of nervousness shows in a person's feet. Jiggling your feet or tapping them is not a good idea. Nor is dangling your shoe. It is distracting and, on a woman, appears to be seductive.

Keep feet flat on the floor, or crossed at the ankles or the knee. But they should look as graceful as possible.

Women should be careful not to broaden their thighs or reveal too much leg when crossing at the knees. Men should avoid the ankle-over-the-knee position, except in very informal meetings. They should also avoid crossing their legs in a feminine manner. It is a definite "turn-off" to most people in business. Men should also take particular care, when crossing their legs, not to push up their trousers and display hairy legs, nor should they make an elaborate display of pulling up their socks.

UNDERSTANDING THE IMPORTANCE OF BODY LANGUAGE

Somewhat paradoxically, technological advances in the last few years have served to place an even greater importance on personal contact. Most top business people are careful to allocate a certain portion of their time to face-to-face contact with colleagues, clients, and customers. We like to meet one another, make eye contact, shake hands, even see one another's offices.

It is easier to get a feeling for a person and how he or she conducts business when you are physically present in the same room. And it is certainly much easier to influence someone and gain control of a situation when you are there in person. It is still easier to say no to a telephone than to a face.

Keep in mind that your body language can change dramatically from one time of day to another and can reflect your own moods, triumphs, or disappointments. Some people are freshest in the morning, and this is the time they project enthusiasm, confidence, and energy. Others wake up more slowly and tend to come alive later in the day.

Once you understand your own metabolism and the effect it has on your body language, you should schedule your day to maximize your peak time. If you are a morning person, schedule your important meetings early in the day; reserve your valleys for the more routine things you have to do, like paperwork or handling correspondence.

□ 20 □
ENTRANCE AND CARRIAGE

Despite a large sign in front of our office complex that clearly states, "No Soliciting," we usually expect to see two or three salespeople who walk into our offices unannounced each day. When salespeople come in, I have no idea how their day has gone, whether they have met with one rejection after another or whether they have achieved their monthly quotas early. But I am keenly aware of how each one is presenting himself or herself at the moment he or she comes through our door.

If the person is savvy enough to put the morning's disappointments behind him and approach me in a manner that says he is confident and in control, that he has something I should hear, then I probably will listen. But if the person's manner is so timid and apologetic that it is telling me he has no reason to be there bothering me, then I am very likely to agree. Or if the individual is obviously angered by a day of frustration and tries to bully his way in, then I am likely to share in the hostility—except that my share will be directed toward the salesperson.

"MAKING AN ENTRANCE"

This term gives us a mental picture of a society queen sweeping into a ballroom; yet all of us make entrances throughout our business day as we enter offices, conference rooms, or meeting halls. And every time we do, someone is watching us, appraising us, sizing us up, and gauging our appearance, confidence, even our intelligence, often within the space of a few seconds. Obviously, then, getting off on the right foot is crucial.

Wrong: The apologetic entrance

Right: The competent entrance

If your entrance is made apologetically, brashly, nervously, or with an air of defeat, then you may already have lost your audience, opportunity, or sale before you even open your mouth.

The key to making a successful entrance is simply believing—and projecting—that you have a reason to be there and have something important to offer. Professional party-crashers are very adept at this. The most successful ones attend all sorts of exclusive functions without the benefit of an invitation. Most of the time they don't know a soul there. Their entree is their self-assured body language that says, in effect, "How dare you question my right to be here?" They communicate, through their body language, that they are important. They can make themselves instantly comfortable in new surroundings.

This is a technique that most business people, particularly those in sales or other public contact positions, would do well to develop—with some modifications. The objective is not free champagne and finger sandwiches but, rather, to make yourself welcome in business situations.

A confident manner is a good start and a worthwhile protective device. Police officers advise people walking alone through unfamiliar neighborhoods to walk quickly and purposefully. Don't look like a victim. This "trick" may not guarantee safety, but it will certainly help. By the same token, you don't want to enter a business situation looking like a victim, like someone to whom people can easily say no.

Facial expressions and body movements are a good indication of how a person is feeling. It is important to be able to read those gestures. No less a social critic than Miss Piggy, in her treatise on life, advised that we "not let the 'chat' out of the bag." And right she is.

Reveal only what will be beneficial to you and your business. Your entrance and the way you carry yourself will set the stage for everything that comes afterward.

THE WRONG WAY

There are several "wrong ways" to come into an office. Perhaps you will recognize a colleague or the salesman who didn't sell you the copier. You may even recognize yourself.

The nervous or apprehensive entrance is the most common "wrong" entrance, and is a trap that you are most likely to fall into on the occasion of a first meeting, an interview for a job you want, or the board meeting that may mean your promotion.

Certainly a little apprehension is normal, even healthy; it can keep you on your toes by sending a little adrenaline flowing through your system so you will be sharp and alert. But don't let this apprehension show in your body language. Hesitant steps, darting eyes or inward motions that will remind your observers of a turtle pulling himself inside a shell won't help you. Be enough of a professional to overcome the fear you have: Make your walk and your carriage say that you have confidence. Hold your briefcase comfortably at your side, never in front of you as a shield—that will make you look frightened or vulnerable.

The fussing and primping entrance is never going to win points. The time to pull yourself together before a meeting or an interview is in the restroom just before you make your entrance. A quick detail check will give you the opportunity to zip, button, straighten, and smooth as necessary. If you make your entrance while you are preening and fussing over your appearance, you will be distracted and so will your audience. You will appear to be unfinished, not quite together. If you know that your appearance is taken care of, you can be comfortable and concentrate on making your audience comfortable with you and the ideas or product you are presenting.

The belligerent entrance starts things off on the wrong foot. No one likes a bully, whether the setting is recess in the third grade or a meeting in a sales manager's office. Never enter an office looking or acting belligerent. Angry, super-aggressive body language is often mirrored by those you meet, who will attempt to place themselves on an "equal" footing to better defend themselves against the negative feelings you are projecting. If you are angry and show it, you will probably anger your audience. If you try to intimidate them, you may succeed at making them uncomfortable. But this is not likely to work to your advantage. Only weak and ineffectual people rely on abusive tactics. You will not be remembered as someone with whom anyone else will want to do business. You may actually make an enemy. Everyone is glad to see a bully get his or her comeuppance.

The worst kind of bully is the one who practices his techniques on receptionists and secretaries. Most executives are very sensitive to this, and will react negatively.

The toy soldier entrance is another mistake. Certainly body movements should be controlled, but the wooden, military stride, coupled with a stern facial expression, is more reminiscent of a wind-up toy. You will look forbidding or, even worse, comical. Relax and your audience will, too.

The Ichabod Crane entrance, clumsy and awkward, is no help in a business situation. If you are naturally inclined to walk with long loping steps and given to extravagant hand and arm gestures that send lampshades crashing or pictures falling off the wall, you need to practice some control. Make yourself comfortable with what you have to say, so you will have no reason to feel awkward. The gawky, nervous manner will make your audience uncomfortable, anxious to get rid of you as quickly as possible.

THE EFFECTIVE ENTRANCE

The person who has confidence in himself or herself indicates this by a strong stride, a friendly smile, good posture, and a genuine sense of energy. This is a very effective way to set the stage for a productive meeting. When you ask for respect visually, you get it.

The right way to enter a room and carry yourself is no mystery. Move your rib cage upward—so that you are not slumping over or pitching forward. Hold your head up. Look at yourself in the mirror and see how you appear. Good posture visually removes pounds. Adjust your stance until you find one that looks comfortable and feels natural. Maintain this carriage while you are walking. Carry your briefcase in your left hand, leaving your right hand free to shake hands. Smile—the smile is a very underrated "tool" that you can use in business. Make it a genuine one that involves your eyes and your whole body. Act as though you are genuinely pleased to be meeting the person you are seeing.

This entrance will do more to make you welcome than any letters of introduction or inside contact. You will have made a good impression. You will look like someone with whom the occupant of the office would like to spend time. And you will be ready to offer your hand in a handshake.

WHEN THE WORST HAPPENS

Most of us have nightmares about walking into an important meeting and falling flat on our faces—literally. Or tripping or stumbling. The best way to handle such a memorable entrance is to recover as quickly as possible with a minimum of disturbance. The longer it takes you to become comfortable again, the longer it will take your audience. Saying something humorous will help you regain your composure and put your audience at ease again. In fact, it can even work in your favor if your recovery is good and your comment is humorously self-deprecating.

□ 21 □

SHAKING HANDS

A handshake is a wonderful business gesture. It is almost universally accepted and understood. It gives you an opportunity to "say" a lot about yourself and to learn something about the person with whom you are shaking hands.

It is very likely the only physical contact you will have in a business encounter. Back-slapping, arm-grabbing and punching all have the potential to offend, but a handshake is almost always appropriate in a business situation. It provides a fairly abstract situation with a beginning and end.

If your handshake is firm and direct, warm and friendly, offered confidently, then you are off to a good start. You have set a cordial tone for a meeting. If the handshake you receive in return is brief and abrupt, offered with no eye contact, then the meeting is already in trouble.

From ancient times, handshakes were used as gestures of peace. A handshake indicated that the hand was open and did not hold a weapon. Originally the clasp was made on the forearm, as a means of making certain that no weapon was hidden in the sleeve. Then the gesture evolved to the hand. By now it is a generally accepted business practice. In a meeting, if everyone except you gets a handshake, be ready for something—probably something you won't like.

In some countries the practice varies. In England the shake is much less firm and the distance between the two shakers is increased. Swedes shake hands much more frequently. Good sense and good manners dictate that you try to make a foreign visitor or colleague as comfortable as possible and modify your handshaking if necessary.

A FAIR SHAKE FOR WOMEN

Back in the era of buggies and bustles, before women had made their mark in the business world, it was considered improper for a man to offer a woman his hand. He had to wait for her to make the offer, then he was expected to give her a delicate half shake. Many women today find that insulting. It is perfectly acceptable, in business situations, for either party to extend the first hand. In fact, the person who extends a hand first actually has an advantage. He or she is establishing control, taking the initiative, being direct—all pluses in a business situation. It is perfectly correct and even very smart for a woman to have her hand out first; this eliminates any hesitation a man might have in offering his hand.

Most fathers whose daughters grew up in the fifties and sixties never expected them to need to know how to shake hands in business. With men composing the majority of the workforce at that time, it made sense. A firm handshake was considered a masculine gesture. Thus, most fathers never taught their daughters.

The upshot is that many women had to teach themselves or had to learn by trial and error.

The other side of the coin is that many men were trained well for offering and accepting handshakes from other men, but find it very awkward to offer or accept a firm handshake from a woman.

In the business world, a man should extend the same procedure and courtesies to a woman that he would to a man. It is not only correct but also desirable for a man to offer his hand firmly to a woman. He is very clearly showing her that he is including her in the same business procedures in which he includes men. A woman should try to discourage any awkwardness by putting her hand out with no hesitation.

TECHNIQUES

A good robust handshake is very American. We like the participation. We like to meet web to web, to include the whole hand. This indicates an openness, a willingness to do business.

When this is coupled with direct eye contact, it indicates that you are friendly, confident, and armed with a purpose. If the clasp is held an extra second, that indicates a little more control. The handshake should be firm, with no pumping.

Male or female, you must never hesitate when you extend your hand. You look meek and uncertain if you offer your hand, then withdraw it, and then offer it again. Hold your hand out firmly and positively with a smile and make strong eye contact. If you aren't sure how your handshake feels to others, then practice with friends.

If your handshake is ever refused, either because someone does not notice your extended hand or because the person chooses to ignore it, simply withdraw your hand discreetly. The embarrassment and the shame, in that case, belong to the person who refused the shake, not to the one who was refused. Besides, you have just gained some valuable information. The person is resentful, angry, or distracted; that may overpower his caution, judgment, or reason. The advantage may be yours.

In perfecting your own handshake, it is important to know what to avoid—as well as how to "read" other people's handshakes.

THE DEAD MACKEREL

No one likes a weak, fishy handshake—it's worse than none at all. It indicates lack of character, enthusiasm, confidence, and just about everything else that is valued in business. No one gives a wet noodle any credibility. It can also indicate hostility or resentment. If you suddenly get a limp handshake from someone who formerly gave you a firm one, that may be a clue that something in the relationship has gone awry. Just as people try to increase the personal space around themselves when they are not comfortable in a situation, so they will place themselves as far away as possible when they are shaking hands, if they feel uncomfortable.

THE BONECRUSHER

This particular shake, most often used by men, is the mark of an insecure person. If the bonecrusher is used on another man, it indicates fear or resentment or extreme competitiveness. Any attempt to be physically assertive is a last resort in business. It is a poor show of force.

THE E.R.A. SHAKE

The man who is still uneasy about the idea of women on an equal footing in business may resort to bonecrusher handshakes to take unfair physical advantage. His shake bruises fingers and crushes rings against tender skin. He is saying, essentially, "You want equal rights, lady? Here's my equal rights handshake." But he is really saying more about his own insecurity than anything else.

THE PROTECTOR

The other extreme is the man who still thinks of women as frail little flowers who might be done in by a firm handshake. He gives a limp, condescending shake that is very like the dead mackerel except that it only includes the fingers. It is demeaning and unsavory.

THE SANDWICH

Someone who is constantly clasping another person's hands with a two-handed shake appears condescending, especially if the recipient's hand is

The sandwich shake . . .

. . . versus the correct shake

turned over horizontally rather than vertically. Handshakes should always be administered vertically. Attempting to turn a hand over is a power play at worst, maternal or paternal at best. This type of handshake takes away the basic egalitarian nature of the gesture.

Remember that this is the way a minister greets his congregation after the service; determine if that's the image you wish to convey. If you do clasp someone's hand with both of yours, make sure it is a gesture showing genuine affection—and remember to keep everything vertical.

THE NO-SHAKE

The no-shake is exactly what it sounds like: a deliberate omission. This is a danger signal to the person who is not offered a hand. If everyone else is being included, be prepared to be ignored or put down during the meeting.

THE GLAD-HANDER

The wild hand-pumper either amuses people or makes them uncomfortable. Madly shaking hands with everyone in sight reeks of phoniness and ulterior motives, which is an especially undesirable trait in someone who is selling.

HAND-TO-HAND COMBAT

Back-slapping and super-aggressive handshakes are reserved only for very good friends. It is amusing to watch two men who wrestle around with their handshake and turn the greeting into a contest of athletic endurance. It can indicate a strong feeling of friendship or one of fierce, understated competition.

THE LAST PHYSICAL CONTACT

Save some impact for the final handshake, the one administered before leaving a meeting. The old last-thing-said, first-thing-remembered saying still applies.

A client of mine who runs a small company decided to purchase a word processor. It was a difficult decision because of the dollar investment. A large part of her decision was based on the fact that the salesperson had spent a great deal of time explaining all the machine's benefits, and the client felt very comfortable with him. However, when the salesman appeared at her office with the contract, he seemed to be in a big hurry. My client was unconsciously looking for signs of assurance that she had done the right thing. But what she received was a perfunctory handshake, a cloud of smoke, and a fleeting smile as the salesman moved on to the next prospect. She felt that she had been had, and it was enough to make her reevaluate her decision. She still bought the processor, but she had second thoughts.

The salesman could have saved himself and my client a lot of trouble had he put as much into his exit handshake as his entrance one.

□ 22 □
MAKING EYE CONTACT

Our eyes give away a lot more information than we realize—but, fortunately, so do everyone else's. We all get a great deal of information from other people's eyes. Most of our descriptions of people include comments about their eyes—"shifty eyes," "piercing eyes," "flashing eyes." They are clichés because they are so apt. The descriptions tell us a lot more than simply the look of someone's eyes.

In the business world, eye contact can give a good indication of position and rank. It is relatively simple to view two people and determine who is the boss and who is the subordinate. The subordinate makes much more eye contact, generally nodding more and showing interest. The superior, though, usually makes less eye contact, looks around the room, even glances through some papers on his desk, without being rude.

In business and social situations alike, eye contact is critical. Without it, we get only fragments of information. It's like talking to someone through a bad telephone connection when you miss every other word.

Consciously or unconsciously each of us forms an initial opinion of someone else based in large part on how the other person communicates with his or her eyes. Particularly in our American culture, it is critical that we make direct eye contact about eighty percent of the time when we are dealing with other people.

Most individuals will gaze more directly when they are listening than when they are talking. So it is important to remember to look at your listener when you are trying to make an important point. It will be a good opportunity to make eye contact and, of course, to gauge the reaction to what you are saying. Looking directly at someone is also almost universally interpreted as a gesture of confidence.

USING EYE CONTACT FOR CONTROL

Most of today's top salespeople have a full understanding of eye contact, and have learned how to use it effectively. All of us have bought things we didn't really want or need just because a salesperson was so good with eye contact; he made us feel included, important. People don't buy products or ideas on the basis of logic. They buy emotionally.

If you are conducting a meeting, it is very easy to use eye contact to control who speaks and who doesn't. When you look at someone, and especially when you nod or show interest, you are giving the speaker permission to talk. If several people are attempting to speak spontaneously, the individual who gets the most direct look will end up with the floor. This works socially, too. If several people at a party are vying for the limelight, look directly at just one person. That individual will feel he or she has been "appointed" the speaker.

Lack of eye contact, on the other hand, can very definitely work against you. When someone does not meet your gaze, it indicates to you that you are being ignored, that who you are and what you have to say are not important. If, during the course of a meeting, eye contact is broken, you had better pick up on that fact immediately and make adjustments accordingly. Someone who is constantly looking at his watch is telling you your time is up. If you feel you are being given short shrift, you can take a direct approach and ask, "Do you have another appointment?" or "Would

Lack of eye contact: Recognize what it means.

Direct eye contact: You have their attention.

you like me to come back another time?" People who continue to bluster along without acknowledging the message are often those who cannot understand why they are not successful, since they certainly say all the right things.

Hiding your eyes behind sunglasses or tinted lenses is not a good idea, unless you have just come from an appointment with your ophthalmologist. Dark glasses give you a sinister look and make you appear to have something to hide. They also deprive you and your client or colleague of eye contact. That is devious and unfair and may backfire.

SINCERE AGREEMENT

Nodding is a good complement to eye contact. It shows a speaker that you are listening and absorbing what is being said and is a very positive way of stating to people that you are on their side. It is a time-saver, since you don't have to interrupt verbally by saying, "Yes, I agree."

Getting your listener to nod is a good way to reassure yourself that you are making an ally, that you are making your point. Likewise, when you are the nodder, remember that the gesture must be done judiciously. You don't want to look like one of those dogs with the bouncing heads in the back of car windows. Yet nodding is a wonderful, rhythmic movement in which everyone in the room can participate. If your boss is presenting some difficult or controversial information, you can show your support by nodding during the session.

If you want to catch the attention of a speaker, use the nodding technique. Anytime I speak I find myself always looking at the nodder in a group of people. This is a common experience for anyone who speaks to large groups. You simply can't help it. The nodders appear to be on your side and have the good sense to agree with you, and that's hard to resist. Visual encouragement is always appreciated.

Nevertheless, too much nodding will seem artificial, or it may appear even to be a nervous habit or a carefully orchestrated snow job.

A client of mine ended up with a car that she didn't need because the salesperson was such an effective nodder. He kept asking questions of her to which she could only reply yes. He nodded and she nodded, and the next thing she knew she was buying a car, simply because it seemed impossible for her to shake her head no in the face of his yes. She felt both foolish and as though she had been conned. And she explained this carefully to the sales manager the next day when she canceled the sale.

Nodding must be sincere or it will backfire.

□ 23 □

BODY POSITIONING: CLOSE ENCOUNTERS

Each of us carries around a "bubble" or personal space, and we are resentful when that territory is invaded.

When we get on an elevator alone, we tend to stand in the center, since we have the entire car to ourselves. Then, when someone else gets in, we move to one side and the new arrival claims the other side. Most of us would feel uncomfortable, even unsafe, if the other person moved in very close and left an entire half of the elevator unoccupied.

When a large number of people ride together on an elevator, most of them tend to look at the lighted numbers above the door, rather than make eye contact with fellow passengers they don't know. They are working to reestablish their individual comfort zones, which have been violated by the crowded conditions. Although they might exchange a pleasantry about the weather with a fellow elevator passenger, more often than not casual conversation ceases when the elevator gets crowded. It's just not comfortable.

On crowded subways, there is very little room for personal space. But anyone who does not want to look like a victim will find a way to squeeze out sufficient space, often using a briefcase or a newspaper to extend his individual area.

Space and territory take on even more importance in places where space is at a premium—New York City, for instance. Not long ago, I was grabbing a quick bite to eat at a New York lunch counter where people were literally shoulder to shoulder. The stools were very close together, and if you were not careful you could easily injure your neighbor simply by trying to get a forkful of chicken salad into your mouth at the wrong time. The management in this particular place had done something that was very clever. It had painted white stripes to delineate each person's eating space. So each of us had a small space we could call our own for the duration of our lunch. Since I'm a nonsmoker, I gently pushed my ash tray over the line to the man next to me, who was puffing away. But he pushed it back indignantly to my side of the line. Clearly, he did not want his space cluttered by anything that belonged to me. He was acutely aware, as was everyone else there, that territory was defined.

Territory and personal space are highly significant in business. The old cliché about keeping someone at arm's length is good advice. Never move closer than an arm's length when you are talking to someone. Many times you will need almost two lengths to keep the conversation flowing comfortably.

For most people the normal business distance is somewhere between three and six feet. It changes, obviously, with the situation or as the number of people increases.

A person's individual territory also extends to his personal possessions. I can remember being very offended when a visiting salesman began picking up items on my desk—a pen, a paperweight, my calendar—as he made his sales presentation. He lost me as a customer the minute he "borrowed" my things without asking.

On the other hand, a smart salesperson will try to involve a prospective customer by handing her a catalog or fabric sample, or perhaps by having her hold one end of a blueprint that was rolled up. This is a smooth and unobtrusive way to gain involvement.

TOUCHING

Generally, rank accords certain "touching" privileges—although great care should be exercised beyond a simple handshake. Yet a boss can put his or her hand on a subordinate's shoulder or punctuate sentences by touching a person on the arm. This is generally done much more frequently by men than women. Some men can carry it off—if it seems genuine. But it can very easily seem patronizing or paternal. It can also communicate sexual overtones, which will not work to your advantage in a business situation.

MEETINGS

The location of a meeting can actually help or hurt you and your cause. Holding a meeting in your office gives you a definitive advantage. It is your turf—*your* desk, *your* chair, *your* pictures, *your* calendar. The things there belong to you. Most people who come in, even if they are your superiors in rank, will be aware they have entered your realm and will accord you certain rights and privileges. You also exert a measure of control in your own office. Very few people have ever been fired in their own offices; that usually happens in someone else's space.

You can usually control the seating if the meeting is in your office, and unless you have a particularly large office with a separate seating area, you will probably be seated in the ultimate power position—behind the desk.

The next best thing to holding a meeting in your own office is to opt for neutral territory—a conference room, an outside meeting place, even a restaurant. When no one person can claim the space, it becomes everyone's property. The smart thing in such a case is to position yourself at the most advantageous place in the seating arrangements.

For example, if you are ever anticipating problems from someone who is going to be at the meeting, sit right next to him or her, rather than across. It is very difficult to argue with someone when you are not in the traditional confrontational position. It even works in domestic situations. If your spouse is angry with you, invite him or her out to dinner and make sure that the two of you are sitting side by side. Breaking down the physical distance also serves to break down some of the emotional distance.

Unless you are ready and willing to debate a business adversary, don't sit directly across from him or her. On the other hand, if you want a direct encounter, that's the way to position yourself.

The head of the table generally belongs to the person in charge. If no one has been appointed to be in charge and if it would be to your advantage to sit there, do so. But remember that all eyes will be focused on you for direction, and you will probably end up running the meeting. Make sure you are ready for that.

If you are really looking for control, spread your notebooks, pens, manuals, and anything else you brought along over as broad an area as possible—without bursting anyone else's bubble. This will give you further claim to the territory.

Territory is also defined vertically. Tall people—like me—are better seated in any meeting. Towering over someone may give you an initial advantage, but that quickly evaporates if the shorter person becomes defensive. People like to be able to make direct and level eye contact with someone they are dealing with. Everyone likes to feel themselves on an equal footing. Regardless of how tall or short we are, most of us are about the same height when seated. If you are tall, be sensitive to those who are not or you will turn an advantage into a disadvantage.

POWER POSITIONING

Once we have positioned ourselves—or have been positioned—in a business situation and have established our personal space, we can turn our attention to power positioning, either using it ourselves or observing how it is used by others.

The key point to remember when you are playing the power game (and we all do) is that you won't always win, even if you do know all the tips and tactics. Occasionally, you will be outclassed or overpowered. But never allow yourself to play the role of victim. Victims are victimized. Even nice people take advantage of them. American business offices are full of frustrated business people who never realize that power begins with themselves and their perceptions of themselves.

To paraphrase Henry Ford: If you believe you have power, then you have it. If you don't think you do, then you don't. This isn't meant to suggest that you should become abusive and domineering; it does suggest that you must believe you have something to contribute, whether it is an idea, product, or service. And that must come through your own body language and your reaction to other people's language.

Some classic postures and tactics have a fairly universal significance that is not hard to read—or to incorporate into your own body vocabulary, if it is to your advantage. Remember, though, that the context of each gesture or pose is as important as the pose itself. Don't just look at individual pieces of the picture; step back and view everything as a whole.

Feet on the desk: This is a very effective way of establishing ownership and position. It can communicate dominance. It is a genuine power position. When a man uses the position with other men, he will come across either as a boss who feels comfortably in control or someone who is unbearably cocky. However, when there is a woman in the room, the gesture takes on an aspect of condescension. If you use a form of body language someone else can't imitate, you are putting that person in a very unfair position and are likely to incur their resentment.

No one likes to talk to the bottom of someone else's shoes.

Smiling: This is one of the most powerful means of communication and one that is generally underestimated in business. Almost everyone reacts favorably to a smile that is genuine. A polite smile that shows no teeth and does not involve the eyes can have an almost negative effect. A nervous smile shows your own vulnerability.

A smile can show that you are in control of yourself, confident; it can make you appear cooperative and agreeable. It can also buy you a precious few extra seconds to size up the situation when you enter a room, so you can avoid creating animosity.

Hands behind the head: This can show a certain amount of relaxed comfort or it can be a definite assertion of power; it depends entirely on the context. In one's own office, the hands behind the head may be a means of stretching or relaxing. In a conference room the same gesture might mean a man is asserting himself as the authority. Again, when a woman is present, the gesture becomes condescending, since this is not a gesture a woman may use comfortably. The cut of most women's clothes usually precludes this—unless she wants to rip the sleeves out of her jacket or send her blouse buttons flying.

Steepling: The simple act of placing the fingertips of either hand together in front of you to form a steeple is a very effective gesture that is rarely offensive and will establish you as someone both evaluative and in control. It's a good counter to aggressive power positioning. The steeple takes its shape from the pyramid, which has been perceived as a source of power from ancient times. It also puts something between you and the person with whom you are speaking, thus distancing you, subtly, from the situation.

There are two types of steeples, the high steeple and the low one. The high steeple is made with the fingertips pointed upward and is the stronger of the two. The low steeple has the fingertips pointing outward toward the person you are talking to and indicates a more open position. People who have positions of power often choose to be photographed in the steeple position. It gives them a certain thoughtful, intelligent look. It can do the same for you. It will also give you something to do with hands—a problem for many people. It is your hands that will quickly give you away if you are nervous or anxious.

This man is projecting a great deal of power and control.

This man is also in control, but appears more receptive.

Glasses perched on the end of your nose: This can be very intimidating. It tends to remind us all of the Miss Crabtree who was our shrewish third-grade teacher. It is easy to feel overpowered or intimidated when someone peers at you over the tops of his glasses, or when someone wears the little half glasses for reading that requires him to look over the top. Lyndon Johnson often wore glasses of that style, and they underscored his power very effectively. If you find yourself being looked at in this manner, be ready to counter it with stronger body language—perhaps a steeple or two. If you are the peerer, realize that you may be coming across negatively—depending upon what the rest of your body language is saying.

Folded arms: Folded arms do not always mean that someone is turned off or has tuned you out, although that is a possibility. Some people fold their arms simply because they are cold; others find it a comfortable position. But if the folded arms are accompanied by a skeptical facial expression, a rigid body, perhaps even narrowed eyes, the message is clear. The person doesn't like you or what you are saying.

READING YOUR AUDIENCE

Gerhard Gschwandter uses colors to indicate the difference in an audience's attitude toward a speaker. Red stands for obvious strong resentment. If you see or sense active resentment, you see red, usually portrayed by a total disregard for making eye contact. You need to stop talking and take quick action. The best thing to do is to put the ball in the other court. Start asking questions, and listen to the answers you get.

If your audience is touching its face, leaning on one hand, or assuming the classic thinker's position, then the group or the individual is in a yellow mood—evaluative but cautious. Keep going. You have your audience's interest and attention.

If your listeners are in a green mood, you have all but closed the deal. The person or group may assume a sprinter position, start nodding energetically, or simply lean forward. This is the time for you to wind up the negotiation, get out the contract, or ask for a verbal commitment. Interestingly enough, this is the point at which most salespeople fail. They continue to rattle on, ignoring the go signals, and actually push the listeners back to the yellow zone by giving too much information or showing insensitivity.

FLIRTING

Usually when a man and woman meet in business for the first time there is a very subtle hint of sexual tension evident, often so slight that it does not register consciously with either party. Once a business relationship is established, the tension disappears fairly quickly.

But flirting is at once a tactic that can be used—usually disadvantageously—and an entire area of body language that demands some sensitivity.

Blatant flirting, whether it is initiated by a man or a woman, is out of place in a business situation. It is particularly dangerous for a woman to use her sexuality or appear to be using it consciously in business dealings. It will lessen her professional stature.

If you're thinking to yourself that this sounds like sexist advice, you are right. This is one of the areas where a man is more equal than a woman. It's not fair, but that's still the way it is. Such flirting won't help anyone, but realistically, a man can get away with more than a woman.

I once worked with a woman who never said a sexy word to any male she met, but her nonverbal message came through loud and clear. Her hair, which fell alluringly over one eye, her sexy stance, and her coy glances all sent out the wrong messages. She told me she was constantly annoyed by men and that she was never taken seriously and she wondered why. She asked my advice.

She didn't necessarily like what she heard—I told her exactly what I thought her body language was telegraphing—but she paid attention, and made some changes, with good results.

SENDING AND RECEIVING MESSAGES

When it comes to body language, you generally receive what you ask for. A positive person gets back a positive response. Negative people receive a lot of grief.

Positive, self-assured people who show enthusiastic but controlled body language in their business dealings energize others around them. Genuinely enthusiastic, confident individuals who value themselves and their time are hard to resist. Everyone likes to be associated with confidence and success. If you act confident and successful, you are more than halfway there.

□ 24 □
MINDING YOUR P'S AND Q'S: CORPORATE ETIQUETTE

Good business etiquette is based on the same principle as good personal or social etiquette: Basically, do what will make other people most comfortable, without compromising your own comfort and health. A generous dash of common sense never hurts either.

SMOKING

Cigarette smoking should be done only in your own office, unless you are in the office of someone else who is smoking. It is not a good idea to smoke in a meeting room or anywhere there are nonsmokers present. Nonsmokers—and I have to include myself among them—have become much more assertive about their rights in the last few years. Many of them will be offended if you smoke without asking.

It's a good idea to have a smoke-eater device in your own office if you do smoke so the odor won't offend your nonsmoking clients and customers.

If you are the nonsmoker in the office of a smoker, you will very likely have to bite the bullet. It really is not advisable to ask someone to refrain from smoking on his or her own turf. You wouldn't make the same request in someone's home, and an office is as personal a place. Possible solutions would be to try to schedule meetings in your office, where you have more control, or to move to a conference room that is larger and allows the smoke to dissipate.

Generally, if someone asks, "Do you mind if I smoke?" you should feel free to say yes, you do mind—unless the person asking the question is your boss or a prospective client. "Thank You for Not Smoking" signs are a little heavy-handed for an individual office unless they are done with some humor.

Smoking can be detrimental not only to your health but to your professional success. Chain-smoking indicates nervousness and in a business negotiation often tips people off that you are overly anxious and concerned. This can prove to be information damaging to your cause.

Cigar-smoking is rude and offensive to everyone except the cigar smoker. Cigars are not a good idea at all; their smell persists long after the cigar has been put out, and their odor is obnoxious even to many cigarette smokers. They should be reserved for solitary meditation or enjoyed with other cigar smokers. Also, a cigar makes an individual look rather smug and self-satisfied, and there is a negative sort of image connected with this cigar-chomping "boss man."

It is particularly difficult for a woman to get away with smoking either cigars or the thin cigarettes with dark paper that look like small cigars. They make her appear to be trying too hard to move into a man's world via the cigar-chomping image.

Pipe-smoking is rarely a good idea for a woman or a man in a business situation, unless you are a professor or psychologist, or it is to your advantage to appear deliberative. If you are in a competitive, fast-paced business, the pipe smoker image is not likely to be a help to you.

Apart from the image they project, pipe smokers can be very distracting in business—with their never-ending cycle of pipe-cleaning, filling, tapping, packing, and lighting, followed by long draws and displays of paraphernalia. Additionally, there are many people who find the odor of pipe tobacco fully as offensive as that of a cigar.

OPENING DOORS AND HOLDING COATS

Much seems to have been made of the who-opens-the-door-for-whom issue, but it is primarily a matter of common sense. Whatever is natural and comfortable is correct; anything that is contrived and awkward is incorrect. Whoever reaches the door first and is least burdened by bags or parcels should open the door. A woman who stops at a door and stands there as though she has just broken her arm is as ridiculous as a man who huffs and puffs, barges ahead, and knocks a woman aside just so he can be courteous and open it for her. The act of opening a door or holding a door should always be interpreted as a kindness and accepted with grace. Many older men were raised with the idea of holding doors open and holding coats, and simply find it hard to change their habit. Opening a door is not a political statement, just simple courtesy, regardless of the gender of the opener.

The "issue" of holding a coat is similar. Many times when I am on a plane, I help a male seatmate on with his coat. It seems silly to stand there as though I am paralyzed while he is struggling with a tangled sleeve.

PICKING UP THE CHECK

There is no reason for this to be awkward, whether the check is to be paid by a man or a woman. If you want to pay, there are several ways to ensure that you get the check. You can always call ahead and make arrangements, or you can simply ask the waiter discreetly to make sure the check is brought to you. A smart waiter or waitress, bringing a luncheon check to a table at which a man and woman are seated, will simply place the check exactly between the two.

If you don't want to pick up the entire check, or don't feel you ought to, ask the waiter ahead of time for separate checks. In a private club, normal procedure dictates that the member will pay the bill. But some clubs are making it easier to divide the check. The Women's Commerce Club in Atlanta, a nice place to take clients, colleagues, or friends for lunch, simply asks members to call ahead and indicate that separate checks are to be given. This ensures that the club gets used more—and the members don't have to pick up the tab all the time.

TELEPHONE ETIQUETTE

The telephone is both a blessing and a curse to the business person. But it is an undisputed fact of business life. Since you are going to have to spend a certain amount of time on the phone, learn to use it effectively. Speak in a clear, firm voice, and don't eat, drink, or chew gum while you talk. Don't mumble or prop the phone between your chin and shoulder while you try to read reports or sign letters.

Don't jangle or shuffle papers on your desk so that the person on the other end of the phone hears a lot of background noise. And don't excuse yourself every thirty seconds to speak to your secretary or a colleague while on the phone. Make your calls brief and to the point.

No matter how bad your day has been, try not to communicate defeat or disgust over the phone. Your telephone image replaces your visual image and is therefore just as important. Here's some additional advice:

- When you answer the phone, do so in a courteous manner. If your secretary has routed the call to you, a friendly "This is Joseph Martin" or "Joseph Martin speaking" establishes a cordial tone and gives the necessary information. It is preferable to a curt "Martin" or "Martin here." If your caller has been identified, always greet him or her by name when you answer.

- When placing a call, always identify yourself—and your firm, if that is appropriate. If you are selling, don't waste people's time by asking them how they are and getting too familiar. If this is the first time you have spoken to the caller, a straightforward "Hello, my name is Sandra Johnson from Apex Business Computers and I would like to speak to Stephanie Hall" is far better than "Hi, this is Sandy. How are you? Nice weather. Is Steffie there?" Also, once Sandra has Stephanie on the phone, a friendly, direct approach presents a far better image than the overly familiar.

PUTTING YOUR HOUSE IN ORDER

I recommend that every business person call his or her own office or switchboard anonymously and see what kind of reception the public is getting. Ask questions in order to get a good idea of how your customers are being treated. There is no point in spending thousands of dollars on an ad campaign to convince the public yours is a friendly, responsive firm if your receptionist offends half the people who call.

If you have a general receptionist and then the call is routed to your secretary, instruct her on how you want your calls screened. Some business people prefer to be open and accessible and will screen their own calls. Others prefer to know exactly who is on the other end.

It is certainly reasonable to want to know who is calling. But if the caller fails to identify himself or herself, he should not get a brusque "Who's calling?" Most callers find this very irritating. If it is essential that you know who is on the line before you take a call, your receptionist should take great pains to be polite. A very courteous "May I tell her who is calling, please?" will probably not be offensive to most people.

However, if your clients or customers call you frequently to purchase your product, it is better not to ask who is calling. Either have the call put straight through or have your receptionist or secretary tell the caller that you are at lunch and ask if she can be of help.

It is particularly rude to make the caller repeat a complicated spiel to a receptionist, a secretary, and finally an assistant. Instruct the people who answer your phone to ask only the questions necessary to route the call properly and save time for everyone.

Whatever the procedure in your office, everyone should have the story straight. There's nothing ruder than being told someone is in, asked to identify yourself, then hearing, "Oh, I'm sorry, he just stepped out." The implication is clearly that the person doesn't want to talk to you.

Recognize that on the telephone, your good manners become your professional image and they need the same consideration and attention that you pay to your wardrobe and your body language.

□ 25 □

THE WAITING GAME: PROFESSIONALISM DURING PREGNANCY

Fortunately, the days when pregnant women were expected to retire discreetly to their knitting as soon as their "condition" became obvious are well behind us. Many women work right up to their delivery dates, and a lot of them actually go to the hospital from the office.

How you look has a great deal to do with how you feel. Obviously, your doctor will be your best guide as to what you can and should do during your pregnancy. If there is ever a time to pay close attention to the basics of good health, this is it.

Being pregnant and looking professional may seem, at times, to be at odds. Too many manufacturers of maternity wear still have the image of the housebound expectant mother who is simply marking time rather than the active professional who is working while she waits—or waiting while she works. But it is entirely possible to maintain your professional image during pregnancy.

It will help if you consider your maternity wardrobe needs in terms of the three trimesters, rather than one long nine-month period. Your appearance will vary greatly over the duration of your pregnancy, and so will your wardrobe needs.

First trimester: For most of this time you will be able to wear clothes from your regular wardrobe; in the third month you will begin favoring the looser garments in your wardrobe—those with some ease in the waist or with adjustable tie belts. By the end of the third month you will feel that you are in something of a clothing twilight zone. Your regular clothes are too tight or uncomfortable, but you may feel a little silly bringing out your roomy new maternity clothes. This is the time to wear unbelted dresses and start to look in the "regular" dress department for convertible outfits.

Second trimester: This is the part of your pregnancy when you will probably be looking and feeling your best. You will, more than likely, have overcome the fatigue and occasional queasiness that characterize the first few weeks, and you may even have acquired the famous "glow" that results when all the hormones start doing their work. Yet you won't stop traffic with the size of your girth. This is the time you will start wearing maternity clothes.

Third trimester: The final weeks of your pregnancy are likely to be the only time when your size might actually be a problem. The amount of weight gained can vary greatly from one woman to another, or one pregnancy to another. The important thing to remember is that it is foolish to worry about *looking* pregnant—of course you look pregnant, if you are six weeks away from delivery. Concentrate, instead, on looking *professional*.

CHOOSING YOUR MATERNITY WARDROBE

Many of the same principles that apply to purchasing a regular business wardrobe will apply to selecting maternity clothes to be worn on the job.

Remember that you are talking about clothes you will be wearing a maximum of six months; so it makes sense to be as budget-conscious as possible without sacrificing quality. You may be surprised to find that maternity clothes, in comparison to regular clothes, are less expensive.

This is because they are made to be worn for a limited time, and because the fit and the tailoring do not have to be as precise. But this will work to your advantage when you are making your selection.

When you are buying maternity clothes, remember that you will not bounce back to your original size after the baby is born. You may need to wear some of these garments for a month or so following the birth. However, I think it is a mistake to buy very expensive maternity dresses with the idea that you can take them in or alter them in some fashion, incorporating them into your regular business wardrobe. Usually a maternity garment is like a bridal gown—no matter what you do to it, it still looks like what it is.

Most of the women I have talked to—whether they are professionals or full-time mothers—say they were so tired of their maternity clothes that they couldn't bear the thought of wearing them any longer than they needed to. There seems to be a psychological association with feeling ungainly and overweight that makes the idea of wearing altered maternity clothes good in theory but not in practice.

FABRIC

Even though your entire pregnancy will span three distinct seasons, you should be able to avoid having to buy "hot-weather" and "cold-weather" clothes. Instead, make your selections, particularly the main items—dresses, jackets, and tailored jumpers—in comfortable, lightweight, seasonless materials. You can utilize some of your regular blouses to coordinate with them (just leave several buttons undone under a jumper). Choose cotton, cotton blends, and lightweight fabrics for blouses. You will find that even if you were once cold-blooded, your body temperature will now seem higher. So avoid heavy, hot fibers.

Your best choices for major garments are fabrics that fall slightly away from your form and have good body of their own—like gabardines, wool crepes, heavy cotton poplins, and some of the better knits. These are much more flattering and more comfortable than clingier materials.

COLOR

It's a good idea to select two basic colors for major pieces in your maternity wardrobe—say, black and tan, or burgundy and gray—just as you would do for your regular wardrobe. You might even stay with the basic colors you already have in your wardrobe, so you will have a wide selection of shoes, scarves, and jewelry to complement them.

Choose your major pieces in darker colors, and use brighter colors—emerald green, bright red, and pink—closer to your face.

FIT

The most difficult thing about selecting maternity clothes is not knowing how large you are going to be in the final weeks of your pregnancy and exactly how the weight will be distributed. Some women simply gain "baby" weight; others gain all over. More than one woman, eight weeks pregnant, has bought an attractive maternity dress that looked very nice on her and fit perfectly, only to find she couldn't get into it three months later. Don't start buying maternity wear until you get some idea of how quickly you will be gaining your weight and where you will be gaining it. And look primarily toward beltless dresses and jumpers, which will accommodate weight gain better than any other style.

Some maternity shops provide a little heart-shaped pillow that you can tie around your midsection to get an idea of what you will look like in the later weeks of your pregnancy. A knowledgeable saleswoman in a maternity shop or department store can be a real help; but don't let anyone talk you into anything that you aren't sure of.

Wherever else you may or may not gain weight, you can count on losing your waistline, having a large abdomen, and probably enjoying a more generous bustline. These are places where you will need room to grow. But it's not likely that your shoulder size will increase drastically. So if you are normally a size 8, don't buy a 14 maternity dress with the shoulder seams hanging down your arms.

Dresses and jumpers present fewer fitting problems than trousers and pants, and they will give you a much more professional look. You may be able to wear a "civilian" dress in a style that has four large front pleats or soft gathers at the neck. Many designers feature the front pleats simply because it is a feminine and slimming look on any woman, not just a pregnant one. Belt the dress until your tummy causes the belt to ride too high. Do remember that your breasts will enlarge and even this style, although it has extra room in the abdomen, may be binding under the arms if your bustline increases too much.

In general, you want to wear your hems a little bit longer than on your regular clothes. You should make sure that any garment you buy has a hem that can be easily let out, particularly in the front. You may also need extra length in your garments during the final weeks of your pregnancy.

Give yourself plenty of room in the armholes and at the neckline, so your clothes will feel comfortable.

STYLES

Your best choices are dresses and tailored jumpers, classically styled. Coat dresses are often a good choice for the first six months. Maternity suits are appearing on the market but they add so many extra layers of fabric across the front that many women look bulky in them. Skirts with tops are reserved for the more informal of industries. They also are less flattering, because they cut you in half and draw attention to your midsection.

Trousers should be avoided for office wear, but for casual wear, a maternity blouse and trousers actually look better than a blouse and skirt.

Don't fall into the trap of looking *cute*. For some reason, too many designers and manufacturers of maternity clothes seem determined to bedeck expectant mothers with excessive lace and ruffles, which do nothing to enhance a business look. A simple tie neckline, or a tailored neckline accented with a scarf, will be flattering because the accent will be on your face. But do keep the look uncluttered or it will make you look very fragile and helpless rather than professional and competent.

Here are some styles and details to look for . . . and some to avoid:

- Pintucking is an excellent means of adding feminine detailing while still staying professional.

- A chemise style (undefined waistline) with several large pleats in the front or a long tunic style top is a good choice. Both are very slimming but still give you room to grow.

- A tailored cardigan style sweater, very tightly knit, can work as a jacket and be a nice addition to a maternity wardrobe. Some women have a dressmaker make them several loose, unstructured jackets to wear with ready-made maternity dresses and jumpers.

- Many pregnant women have shopped successfully at import stores for Oriental wrap-style dresses and tops that can work well as maternity clothes. Others have found good buys at resale shops.

- Of course, T-shirts that say "Baby" or "Under Construction" are inappropriate anytime—and in poor taste as well.

ACCESSORIES

Most of your simple jewelry—small gold earrings, a plain necklace or bracelet, even a deftly tied silk scarf—can be used to vary your maternity wardrobe. Just remember it is even more important not to overdo it or clutter yourself up with baubles and bangles.

The medium-heeled pumps in your wardrobe will look right with your maternity clothes and give you a longer look. But you might, for comfort, want to invest in a pair of shoes with lower, sturdier heels, particularly if your legs and feet swell. You may also be forced to purchase several pairs of shoes larger than your normal shoe size if swelling is a serious problem.

The key to choosing shoes is to remember proportion. If you wear high, spiky heels in your eighth month of pregnancy, you will probably look like some large, exotic bird. It is better to choose lower heels. Boots are never a good choice for a professional look, and this is especially true during pregnancy. Aside from the fact that your feet may be inclined to swell, making the boots very uncomfortable, the proportion will work against you. The heavy boots and a large midsection will make you look like a caricature of a World War II field marshal.

Many of the accessories and some of the blouses may come from your regular wardrobe.

Suggested Maternity Wardrobe

- [ ] Black jumper
- [ ] Burgundy jumper
- [ ] Gray jumper
- [ ] Gray dress in small print
- [ ] Burgundy dress in small print
- [ ] Blue dress
- [ ] Bright turquoise blouse
- [ ] Bright emerald-green blouse
- [ ] Crisp white blouse with stand-up collar
- [ ] Red, unconstructed jacket
- [ ] Black, well-tailored cardigan without buttons
- [ ] Three oblong silk scarves, incorporating variations of red, black, burgundy, gray, turquoise, and emerald
- [ ] One pair black business shoes
- [ ] One pair burgundy business shoes

UNDERPINNINGS

Although you will certainly encounter salespeople more than willing to sell you an entire maternity lingerie wardrobe, first see what you already have that you can use.

A good bra is essential for support. If your regular size and style becomes too small, and if you are planning to nurse your baby, go ahead and buy a couple of good, sturdy cotton nursing bras. They will serve you well after the baby is born, and are quite comfortable and easily adjustable.

Half slips will be easier to manage than full ones. Your regular slips, perhaps with an extra piece of elastic added, should work, or your regular style several sizes larger. In the final weeks of your pregnancy, particularly if your maternity clothes are lined, you may want to omit a slip entirely.

Rather than paying a premium for maternity hose, many women simply buy larger "queen-size" versions of their regular brands. Elastic support hose will offer some extra support. In business, never skip the panty hose. Depending on your size, your regular bikini-cut pants or several pairs in a larger size may work well for you throughout your pregnancy.

The main point is to not buy a lot of maternity lingerie until you actually need it. One professional woman dutifully stocked up on super-size maternity panty hose that she still hadn't grown into by the time she left for the hospital.

HAIR AND MAKEUP

Make a special effort to keep your makeup fresh and your hair attractive. Because wardrobe possibilities will be limited, experiment with some new makeup color and try a new haircut with some highlighting. Enjoy the benefits of a more glowing complexion and shinier hair.

BODY LANGUAGE DURING PREGNANCY

Your body may broadcast the news that you are a mother-to-be; but your body language should say professional. It is doubly important during this time that your handshake be firm, your carriage confident, and your smile genuine. If you look tired and uncomfortable, your colleagues and clients will probably be uncomfortable, too. If you act "normal," then they will respond in the same fashion.

When you are sitting down, don't sprawl all over the softest chair in the room. It's almost impossible to get up gracefully. A straight chair will be the most comfortable and the easiest to navigate, especially if you are very large.

Try to avoid an exaggerated pregnant walk—back arched, legs splayed, hands supporting your back. That will call undue attention to your size and won't actually make you feel any better.

In your own office, you may make certain minor concessions to your comfort—a small footstool under your desk to rest your feet, perhaps a desk chair that will give you more back support. But make certain these things are discreet.

If you are more than three or four months pregnant, it is unrealistic not to expect people to react to your condition. You should bring up the subject first in a positive manner. If you don't, your clients or coworkers may spend their time concentrating on how to broach the subject, rather than the business at hand. As long as you don't make people uncomfortable with your pregnancy, you may find it actually creates allies.

You may find yourself the recipient of some unexpected kindnesses, from both men and women. Accept them gracefully and in the spirit they are intended. The impending birth of a baby often brings out the best in everyone. Their concern is much more likely to be prompted by positive feelings than any desire to treat you as though you are incompetent.

ANNOUNCING YOUR PREGNANCY

As soon as you are certain that you are pregnant, you should inform your boss. He or she should not hear about your condition through the office grapevine. When you approach your boss, you should have a pretty clear idea of how long a leave you will need and be ready with some suggestions for handling your responsibilities or clients in your absence.

FIRST IMPRESSIONS: YOUR INTERVIEW IMAGE

An interview is always an opportunity—to get a job, to find out about a particular industry, or simply to practice your interview skills. If you are fresh out of school or have not been job-hunting for a long time, seize any interview opportunity and take advantage of it, even if you are not sure you want a particular job. Consider it a dress rehearsal for the one that you do want. Any invitation to come for an interview is a point in your favor, a positive sign, whether it is a preliminary visit with the company's personnel director or the prelude to a final selection. Something about you has impressed someone. It may be your resume, your experience, your demeanor, even your telephone voice or a letter you wrote. Use the opportunity to your best advantage.

DRESS THE PART

How you look and present yourself at the interview is crucial. Take no chances in your appearance. Dress as well as you can. An office manager from a very well-known ad agency who does a lot of hiring said, "When I walk into the lobby and meet someone who has come in to interview for a job, I don't know for certain if I am going to hire him, but I do know if I am *not*. People usually get sloppier in their appearance instead of better after they have been hired. Not always, but a lot of times. It's kind of a first-date syndrome—you put your very best foot forward, you are at your apex visually. So if a new candidate can't even satisfy the minimum appearance requirements on an interview, the day-to-day appearance will be a real problem."

A suited look is an excellent interview choice for a man or a woman. Don't fall into the trap of trying to act nonchalant or dressing down to indicate that you don't need the job. That sort of attitude is counterproductive. Project as well as you can every time.

FOR MEN

In an interview situation, opt for a conservative look. A solid-colored suit in a dark gray or navy blue, worn with a white shirt and a burgundy striped or foulard tie is completely correct, especially for the first interview. You can dress less formally, in a navy blazer and contrasting trousers, on subsequent interviews if that seems appropriate. But impress them the first time with your authority and control.

However, if you are interviewing with a casual company where you are certain that everyone will be wearing short-sleeved shirts, usually without a jacket, then you are better wearing a blazer and trousers to the initial interview. You want to impress them, not overwhelm them.

Don't wear pocket handkerchiefs or jewelry other than a wedding band or a simple signet ring and a traditionally styled watch. A college ring with a large stone emblazoned with your fraternity insignia is something to be proud of, but not worn on an interview if you are fresh out of school. It will align you too closely with college and not with the business world. If the interviewer is interested in your extracurricular activities, he or she can look at your resume.

Shave off your beard, preferably a week ahead of time so you can get used to the new look and once again condition your face to daily shaving. Give your mustache a cool, critical appraisal. Does it really make you look better? If you decide to keep it, make certain that it is neat and well-trimmed. Have it done professionally for a really important interview. Don't wear cologne, it may offend your future employer.

Pay attention to details. Pay to have your interview shirt starched and pressed. You will feel more efficient and your appearance will greatly improve. Wear black or navy over-the-calf socks and well-shined black shoes, in a lace-up or slip-on style. Make sure that the heels are not run-down. Don't wear penny loafers; you don't want to give the impression you are fresh off the campus and wet behind the ears.

It is a good idea to bring along extra copies of resumes or any portfolio information you may have. If you are used to carrying a briefcase, bring it to the interview. If you feel awkward and unnatural with one, carry a nice leather note pad. Borrow one if you need to. Also borrow a gold or silver pen if you don't own one. It will look more impressive than a plastic one with teeth marks.

FOR WOMEN

The safest choice is a matched solid suit in black, gray, burgundy, beige, or navy. Wear it with an interesting blouse in a color that is flattering to you: a solid red with a black suit, or a burgundy foulard print with a gray suit. Select a stickpin for your lapel or make sure that your blouse has an interesting neckline—a stand-up collar or an asymmetrical tie. Jewelry should be quiet and simple: gold or pearl earrings, no more than one ring on each hand, and a simple watch.

No sorority or fraternity pins or rings for women either. The fraternity and sorority rah-rah, cavalier attitude has been known to turn off business people and it is not worth the risk. However, once you have established yourself in the business world, it may just become a conversation piece. But wearing it on an interview if you are fresh out of school will align you too much with potentially unacceptable college values.

Wear neutral-toned hosiery and medium-heeled shoes with a closed toe: black, navy, or deep burgundy are good colors.

Select either a purse or an attaché case—but not one of each. An attaché case is better if you are used to carrying one. Make sure it is leather or a good imitation and properly scaled to your size. Should you feel overwhelmed by a briefcase of any kind, select a leather note pad. If you do choose a purse, make certain it works with the rest of your outfit. It should be large enough to carry the things you need but also small enough so you don't look overstuffed. Stay as tailored in styling as possible. Bring a gold or silver pen as an unobtrusive way to show your professionalism.

Your makeup should be fresh, well-blended and understated. Don't wear any fragrance. It is not worth risking the possibility of a sneezing interviewer who is allergic to cologne. If your hair is past shoulder-length, cut it or wear it up.

PLAN AHEAD

Both men and women should plan ahead for any contingencies. Be sure your raincoat is clean and pressed and your umbrella is all in one piece, in case it is raining. And do shake out both the coat and the umbrella in the building lobby, so you don't go dripping into the office. In fact, see if there is a place in the lobby of the building where you can check your raincoat and umbrella so you won't have to carry them to the interviewer's office. Depending on where you live, allow yourself an extra fifteen or thirty minutes to get wherever you have to go in the rain; inclement weather always slows traffic.

Arrive at your destination fifteen minutes early, so you have time to locate a restroom and do a detail check (teeth free of food particles or lipstick, makeup fresh, fly zipped, tie straight, etc.). Don't primp in the elevator—you may find yourself riding up with the person with whom you will interview. If his first introduction is watching you brush dandruff from your shoulders, spray your breath, and blow your nose, the impression you make is not likely to be favorable. You won't project much in the way of confidence or consideration for others.

If you are doing a lot of interviewing, make a note on your calendar of what you wore to which interview. You probably have one outfit that you like best, but you don't want to wear it back to the second or third interview and create the impression that you own only one suit or dress. Generally, for men or women, two good suits should get you through a round of interviews and allow you to vary the look sufficiently through accessories. But if you own only one good suit, stick with that rather than wear marginal outfits. Wear a different shirt and tie or a different blouse. If an outfit doesn't fit or is inappropriate, you won't be comfortable and this will show.

Don't wear a new suit, dress, or pair of shoes for the first time to an interview. Be sure you have tried everything out beforehand, or you may be unpleasantly surprised to discover that the zipper doesn't zip, the hem ravels, the trousers are too short, or the shoes pinch. Women shouldn't try a new hairdo that may come apart during the interview.

Strive to be comfortable and show you are at ease in your surroundings. Try not to appear stiff. You want to project confidence in your ability, your appearance, and your experience. If you know you look good, you will feel good and your body language will communicate your confidence.

BE PREPARED

The Boy Scouts have it right: Preparation is important. Don't stop with your appearance; do your other homework as well before the interview. You should have your resume in good shape. It should be neat, concise (not more than two pages) and positive in tone, stating your education, experience, and qualifications. But don't lie. Recruiters are becoming weary and wary of verbose, overblown resumes. There are companies and individuals who will write your resume for a fee. Approach these with caution: The results often sound contrived or too obviously follow a formula. You may be better off asking someone in the business world to read and evaluate your resume and make specific suggestions. Have it neatly typed and copied. Review it periodically and revise when necessary. Don't let it date you. If you are twenty-two years old, it may be appropriate to indicate that you were vice-president of the student body at your college, but if you are forty, mentioning the same office will convey the impression that you haven't done anything important since that time.

You are better off omitting any religious or political information from your resume, unless you are applying for a position with the Fellowship of Christian Athletes or the Republican party, and you are very sure about what they are looking for. Both topics have a great potential to backfire. It's acceptable to list hobbies or outside interests on a resume, especially if they relate to the company in any way, but keep your descriptions brief.

Even if you have supplied the company recruiter or personnel office with a copy of your resume, you ought to bring along several extra copies to leave with other individuals you may talk to in the office. The more people who have your resume, the more people will have you in mind.

If the firm you are applying to has a standard application form, fill it out and ask if you can attach a copy of your resume. Never write "See Resume" on an application form. But some firms use the same standard form for people who uncrate boxes at the loading dock as for salespeople; so your resume, which you have prepared to present your strengths, will work for you.

Before you go on an interview, learn as much about a company as you possibly can. If you know someone who works there, ask a lot of questions. Find out what the office is like, who will be interviewing you. If possible, see the office first. Perhaps you can drop off a resume or pick up an application. Even if you see only the receptionist, you will at least get a feel for the office. Is it all high-tech chrome and plexiglass, with a super-efficient receptionist? Is it cluttered and friendly, with a motherly type who has a box of homemade cookies on her desk? Or is the atmosphere formal, complete with mahogany furniture, Oriental carpets, and a Saks Fifth Avenue–style receptionist?

If you can, talk to the receptionist. If she likes you or remembers you, she can be helpful in putting through your phone calls or making sure you get through to the person you want, rather than an assistant who is simply going to give you the runaround.

While you are in the office on your scouting trip, notice how people are dressed. If things seem very informal, you should scale down your power look. A man might want to wear a tan suit, or a blazer and contrasting trousers. A woman might choose a dress instead of a suit.

Make sure you know something about the industry or the firm itself. You will need to do some research on each industry before you talk to the personnel director. If you are applying for a position selling software, it's a good idea to know what type of software the firm sells and what computers it is compatible with. If you are interviewing with a public company, get a copy of its quarterly and annual reports. Go to the library and see if it has been written up in business publications.

BEFORE THE INTERVIEW

- Practice interviewing in front of the mirror and analyze your body language. What are your strengths and your weaknesses, and what can you do to improve them? Ask several people you trust about the effectiveness of your handshake and the directness of your eye contact.

- Try to anticipate some likely questions: Where do you want to be in five years? What makes you think you can handle this job? How does your experience qualify you? Describe your work history. What can you offer us?

- Be ready for some unusual questions. Sales recruiters often look around the room, then pick up an ash tray or a paperweight and say, "Sell this to me." Be ready to sell it.

- Have good, solid explanations ready for any embarrassing gaps in your resume. Keep them short and simple, but specific. Above all, don't be apologetic, even if you have been unemployed or underemployed for several months. The man or woman who is questioning you probably has a couple of lean periods in his or her own resume too. Simply state that you wanted to take time off to take additional training or that you were traveling, or working as a consultant, or trying your hand at writing, or spending time with a new baby. Just answer directly and don't hedge.

DURING THE INTERVIEW

- Remember that your contact with the interviewer may be brief. Make every second count.
- Walk confidently into the interview room: Hold your head up and offer a firm handshake.
- Listen carefully to what the interviewer says, and watch his or her body language. Take your direction from it. Don't get so busy formulating your next answer that you fail to pay attention.
- Lean forward when you are talking and nod occasionally, to show your interest and attention. Make eye contact. More jobs are lost from lack of eye contact than from lack of experience.
- Try to control any nervous gestures like hair-twisting, nail-biting, tie-straightening, and pen-clicking. Do not chew gum and don't smoke, even if the interviewer does.
- Be respectful of the interviewer's territory. Don't spread your briefcase contents all over the desk, flip the calendar around, pick up photographs of a spouse and children, or borrow a pen.
- Do show enthusiasm—that's a very valuable business commodity.
- And smile. That is a very underestimated "ploy," but one that is quite effective. Project yourself as someone nice to be around.

Everyone is nervous in an interview; try not to let it show.

- Insofar as possible, be yourself. If you have a natural sense of humor, don't be afraid to let it show. You shouldn't try to be a stand-up comic, but don't be afraid to relax.

- Make your attributes work for you; don't apologize for them. If you are young, don't feign a pose of jaded worldly wisdom. Your youthful enthusiasm and optimism—as long as it doesn't translate as immaturity—can be an asset. If you are older, you have experience and maturity to sell. Make them work for you.

- Avoid using slang and jargon in an attempt to impress an interviewer with your inside information on his industry. Unless you are in the same field, this is likely to backfire.

- Ask permission to take notes during the interview. If you do so, do it judiciously, so you won't break valuable eye contact.

- If you have a choice, you will want to set up the interview in a neutral setting, rather than the office of the personnel director or recruiter. A conference room, a special office set aside on a college campus, or a rented hotel suite are neutral choices. You will feel more at ease here than on the recruiter's turf.

- If you decide, during the interview, that you aren't interested in the job or the company, try not to communicate your negative feelings. A job offer, no matter what the source, is a guaranteed ego-boost.

- No matter how badly you need the job, don't let it translate into desperateness. Eagerness is good; desperation isn't.

- Remember, the whole interview process is an important one, worth preparing for and taking seriously. Recognize that your professional image will give you a distinct and immediate advantage.

□ 27 □

SPECIAL IMAGES
FOR SPECIAL OCCASIONS

Sooner or later every business person's calendar will turn up an occasion that is a little out of the ordinary, a departure from the regular business routine. Each of these will demand special care and preparation.

THE BUSINESS "SOCIAL" FUNCTION

Don't kid yourself; the emphasis is on the *business*, even if the clock says it's after working hours. Whether you are attending a cocktail party, reception, or open house at a client's home or office, you are there because of your business ties and you are representing your company. That doesn't mean you can't have a good time. But it does mean you have to make certain that your dress and demeanor are professional.

If you are invited to a function that starts between 5:00 P.M. and 6:00 P.M., then the presumption is that you will come by from the office. Thus, your regular business clothes are appropriate. Certainly you might want to freshen up a little bit—men might take the time to shave, women might reapply their makeup. A fresh shirt or blouse could be in order, but these

267

occasions are pretty much extensions of your business day and a too-dressy "cocktail party" look would be overdoing it.

If the function begins after 6:00 P.M., even if no particular attire is specified, it's safe to assume that a little dressier look is in order. For both men and women, it is perfectly possible to take your regular business attire and simply spice it up a little.

FOR MEN

Wear a clean, crisp white shirt and your most elegant silk tie, with a dark solid or pin-striped suit. Or, if you prefer a more dressy, less officelike look, wear a dark navy or black velvet jacket with contrasting trousers. Then add a solid silk pocket handkerchief. Dark socks are correct, but leave your wing tips at home and wear a lighter slip-on style, which is more appropriate for evening. Don't wear tweeds, plaids, or very soft wools to an evening gathering unless you are sure it's very informal.

FOR WOMEN

The easiest way to dress for an after-hours function is to wear a very vividly colored camisole—emerald green, bright red, or deep pink—with your best black business suit. The change from blouse to camisole gives the suit an elegant sophistication appropriate for an evening look. Replace your daytime pumps with lighter, strappy sandals, and trade in your no-nonsense purse or your attaché case for a small evening bag. Another attractive alternative is a nice silk business dress worn with an evening belt, sandals, and a small satin evening bag.

If these sound like relatively conservative options, the reason is that you are still "at the office," no matter where the business function is held. Save your sex goddess looks for a strictly social occasion. Don't show cleavage or wear anything too tight or too revealing, unless you want to be Topic Number One at the water cooler for the next six months.

FORMAL AFFAIRS

If the invitation says black tie, the gathering is a formal one requiring tuxedos for men, and for women, a true evening outfit.

A man who attends formal functions only infrequently will probably choose to rent a tuxedo for the evening. Make sure you deal with a reputable rental operation that is careful in taking measurements. Always try on the tux and shirt and check carefully to make sure the tie and suspenders are provided. Most rental shops will not starch the shirt, so it is a good idea to afford yourself enough time to have it professionally done at your cleaners.

If you attend more than three formal functions a year, you may consider the purchase of a tuxedo—a very simple, conservative, classically cut black one, since it will probably outlast you. No high-fashion styles or pastels, unless you are headlining in Las Vegas. Having your own tux will save a great deal of time at the rental shops.

When a woman selects her dress for a formal affair, local custom, the weather, even current fashion will dictate whether a short dress or a long one is most appropriate. If the affair is a dinner or reception, usually it is a matter of personal choice—with a shorter dress more versatile and easier to accessorize than a long one. It is also safer because you will never appear overdressed.

But, again, keep your selection on the conservative side. Think of looking elegant and in excellent taste rather than sexy. You don't need to appear Puritanlike, but be wary of baring too much neck, back, or breast. Don't wear an extremely short skirt or a long one that is slit up to the hip. Remember the guys at the water cooler on Monday morning.

By all means, though, try more glamorous makeup and a more sophisticated evening hair style—perhaps something upswept if you are used to wearing your hair in a pageboy at the office.

BODY LANGUAGE AT BUSINESS FUNCTIONS

When you are attending a business social function, keep your body language on the conservative side. Women should not walk or carry themselves in a seductive manner, nor call attention to their cleavage. They should never drape themselves over a man—whether he is an escort, husband, or coworker.

By the same token, men must be aware of inappropriate touching—arms around the waist or shoulders. Sexual or paternal behavior is inappropriate and compromising.

ALCOHOL

Whatever the occasion, remember to stay well within your drinking limit. Many business people make it a practice not to drink at all when they are "on duty." If you decide not to drink, don't be moralistic about it and draw attention to the fact that you are sipping soda. No one really appreciates a teetotaler at an office party, unless one is discreet about it.

On the other hand, don't force a drink on a coworker. No one should ever be made to feel uncomfortable for not drinking.

It's not fair, of course, but a man is more quickly forgiven for becoming drunk than a woman.

YOUR PROFESSIONAL PHOTOGRAPH

Every business person should have on hand a recent black-and-white glossy photograph of professsional quality. These are essential for membership rosters, company brochures, in-house newsletters, local newspapers, and business publications. Very often organizations that ask a business person to speak will want to publicize the presentation in their own newsletter and the local paper. A business publication that requests an article or guest column will usually ask for a photograph too. Don't blow your professional image with a fuzzy snapshot.

Unfortunately, too many people wait until the last minute to have a picture taken. It is much better to be prepared and have one on file. For most business purposes, black and white is sufficient; five by seven is the best all-purpose size, although three by five is usually acceptable. A head-and-shoulders shot is generally all that is required.

SELECTING A PHOTOGRAPHER

A business photograph must be done by a professional photographer. You should always see a photographer's work before you commit yourself. Ask colleagues or business associates for recommendations. A large corporation may have a photographer on staff. If your firm has a public relations office, ask them for recommendations.

Some photographers are willing to come to your home or office and set up the lighting; but this is a time-consuming process, and you will pay extra for it. You will usually get a better photograph by taking the time to go to the photographer's studio.

Not every good professional photographer has a glitzy address and a studio right out of *Architectural Digest*. In fact, commercial photographers need a lot of room to store props and equipment and they frequently rent studio space in industrial areas or warehouses. Judge the photographer by his work, not his surroundings. However, do expect a certain amount of organization and cleanliness.

Price will vary according to your location and the photographer's experience. Expect to pay a *minimum* of twenty-five to fifty dollars for a sitting, but don't be surprised if the tab is closer to one hundred dollars. You will usually receive for this amount ten different proofs from which you can choose one or two finished photographs. If the ten proof shots are technically well done, yet you simply don't like the way you look, you can expect to pay for having them retaken. If there were technical problems or the film or the lighting was at fault, then the photographer should redo them at no extra charge. Feel free to discuss price prior to the sitting, so you have a clear understanding of what you are buying and what your obligations are.

A WORD ON RETOUCHING

A certain amount of retouching can be done on photographs and for this there should be no additional charge. Crow's-feet can be minimized and shadows under the eyes or skin imperfections can be erased, but don't go overboard. Certainly the photograph should present you at your best, but you don't want it to appear as though it were taken ten years ago. Most photographers will use a soft focus on their lens, to diffuse the light. This often eliminates the need for much retouching.

When retouching is in order, the negative itself will be retouched so that every photograph has the improvements. You are paying for the sitting and the prints you order. The negative will usually remain the property of the photographer; he will keep it on file, and you can reorder from him.

Have your photograph taken when you are not in a rush, in case it needs to be reshot. You should allow two or three weeks for the final copies.

WHAT TO WEAR

Bear in mind the need for contrast—from hair to clothing to background. Request a simple background, but never use studio paneling. It looks too dark and often appears cheap. Furthermore, the finish on most wall paneling creates a glare. Don't use an outdoor or natural background for a business shot. And remember to select clothing that will not blend into the background.

Medium tones and colors are best for black-and-white photographs; blues and grays always photograph well. Keep the lines of your clothes very classic and very simple. Both men and women should wear a jacket for a business photo. Men should wear a white shirt contrasted to a medium-dark suit. Women, however, should avoid wearing white next to their faces. Brighter colors will be more flattering to skin tones. Black women should wear a color that is slightly lighter than their skin.

Patterns should be kept very small—on a man's tie or a woman's blouse—and jewelry held to a minimum. For a head-and-shoulders shot, a man should display no jewelry, and a woman nothing more than simple gold or pearl earrings.

Women should wear their usual makeup, but applied with a slightly heavier hand, since the lights will wash out your skin tone. Use more cheek color and more eye color than normal, and select a clear red lipstick with lip gloss on top. It is not necessary to have your makeup professionally done, because the result may be unnatural and make you seem contrived.

Most people look fresher in the midmorning: eyes are brighter, beards are freshly shaven, and puffiness is minimized. This is the best time to schedule a photo session.

Never have a haircut the day of your photo session. Men should have their hair cut about three days before the session; women should have cutting, perming, or coloring done at least a week before, so it will settle in and you can feel comfortable with it. A man should shave no more than two hours before his portrait.

Glasses can cause a glare, but you can borrow a pair of frames with no glass in them from your optometrist, or leave your glasses off entirely. If you do, be sure to remove them several hours ahead of time so there will be no red indentations on your nose or under your eyes.

CAPTURING YOUR PROFESSIONALISM

You will look best if you look straight into the lens. Gazing dreamily off to the side is too reminiscent of a high-school yearbook picture. Arrange your face in a comfortable expression—you might even practice in front of a mirror. You don't want a big grin, since that will make your eyes look small, your face crinkle up and your mouth look too wide. A pleasant look, with a slight smile and brightened eyes, is very effective. Unless your teeth are very unattractive, you ought to show them. If you are having a full-length photo taken in which your hands are going to show, be wary of props. Don't hold a book or clasp your hands in a way that does not seem natural to you.

TELEVISION APPEARANCES

The proliferation of television talk shows and expanded news coverage means TV stations and program producers are looking for knowledgeable people who can talk on a great variety of subjects. It is no longer essential that you be a starlet launching a recording career or an aging actor trying to make a comeback; more and more "ordinary people" are being drafted to appear on television to talk about their work or their special interests. It can be a valuable experience that means good exposure for you and your company and even a nice star-for-a-day feeling.

If you haven't done a TV show before, you may be surprised at how informal everything is. You probably won't have much preparation, other than a telephone conversation with an assistant producer who will offer a very general outline of what will be expected of you. There will probably be no elaborate makeup or wardrobe crew to help; in fact, you'll find everyone on the set so preoccupied that the most you can hope for is to be informed if your fly is unzipped.

So, by way of preparation, try to watch the show several times before you go on, to get an idea of the format. You can probably figure out what some of the most likely questions will be, and you might prepare some short answers—not monosyllables, certainly, but no "Let me start back in 1956 when our company was founded" either.

It's a good idea to practice sitting in front of a mirror to find your best angle and best body positioning. Find a place to put your hands—one that looks natural.

The need to exercise courtesy toward the crew and producers can not be overstated. Top stars are always as courteous and charming to the camera people as they are to the host and hostess. Making friends with all the people who can influence the way you will appear on the tube is just good sense. If your company manufactures any consumer products, bring along at least twelve samples to be passed out at the end of the show. And don't forget to write thank-you notes to the host, hostess, producer, and director.

WHAT TO WEAR ON TV

In all likelihood, you have been invited because you are an authority on some subject; so your clothes should convey that "authority" message—with a few concessions to the cameras and the lighting.

Men should wear medium to dark solid color suits—anything in medium blue or gray is a good choice. Stay away from white or very light tan suits. Avoid glittery jewelry, especially lapel pins, since they will be very distracting. The viewer will concentrate more on the pin than on you and what you are saying. Avoid a stark black-and-white combination, since this is hard for the camera to handle. Don't go any darker than a dark gray. A solid color shirt—white or blue—is a good choice. A bright burgundy tie shows up well, but make certain that prints are very small and regular; stripes should be very discreet. Wing tips appear too heavy on TV; a lighter slip-on shoe is a more attractive style.

Women should wear either skirted suits or dresses with jackets. This gives a more finished look and the jacket has the advantage of providing a place to conceal the microphone. Skirts should be pleated or dirndl, so they cover your knees when you sit.

A woman's suit or suit jacket can be medium or dark toned but it should stop short of black. Dresses or blouses should be in deep, warm tones. Blue is universally flattering. Avoid stark white, since that causes a glare. Red is a good choice for a blouse, as are apricot, peach, cerise, or maroon. Wear a minimum of jewelry and select pearls or nonglittering stones. Wear only netural-toned hosiery and medium-height shoes with a closed toe.

MAKEUP FOR TELEVISION

More than likely you'll be doing your own makeup. Women should make themselves up in much the same fashion as for a photography session. Use your normal makeup, but more heavily applied, especially on the eyes, lips, and cheeks. Shiny and greasy skin is unattractive on television, so use powder for a mat look. However, a shiny mouth is attractive, so do wear lip gloss.

Even men will look better with a coating of mat powder. In Dan Rather's book, *The Camera Never Blinks,* he told of the late CBS photojournalist Laurens Pierce, who once said that the hardest thing he had to do, when covering confrontations during the Civil Rights Movement, was to stand before an angry crowd and apply his pancake makeup.

You don't need to go this far, but a little mat powder won't hurt.

ON CAMERA

Remember that the camera is the eyes of the audience. When it is focused directly on you, and the red light is on, talk to it. Look at it directly.

Your posture is important. The camera will accentuate any slumping. Women should be particularly conscious of keeping their knees together. Find a comfortable sitting position so you will appear relaxed.

Always take a detail check before you go on television. Smile, and check your teeth for food particles or lipstick; make sure your tie is straight.

Then relax—and enjoy the limelight.

SPEAKING ENGAGEMENTS

Anytime you stand at a podium, addressing a crowd of people, you want your clothing and your body language to convey a clear message of authority—to convey that you are someone who has something to say. Someone who is worth listening to.

Opt for a strong look—solid or pin-striped suit for men and women. Men can select their shirts and ties with an eye toward the more specific audience. Go the whole nine yards for your company board of directors, with a crisp white shirt and burgundy foulard or striped tie. But if you are talking to a group of volunteers about fund-raising, you can wear a pale blue or beige shirt and a striped tie.

Women should wear a white silk blouse and a black suit for the maximum authoritative look, or they can soften the effect with a red or deep pink blouse. But pay attention to the way you look. People are going to see you before they hear you and they will be making mental evaluations of you.

Your speaking manner should be authoritative but natural. Don't read your speech, but have a thorough grasp of your material. Remember that body language is important. Stand up straight, look confident. If you don't project the air of someone who knows what he or she is talking about, then your audience will tune you out. Speak in a strong, clear voice.

Pay attention to your audience and how they are reacting. If they seem to be drifting away, be able to alter your format. Remember *they* invited *you* to speak, because they assumed that you had something worthwhile to say. Show them that you do.

□ APPENDIX □

The following wardrobe inventories have been designed for you to specifically chart every business garment in your closet. List each item by color in the appropriate category. New wardrobe combinations will become apparent, as will specific needs. Use this guide to help you determine your next five purchases.

WARDROBE INVENTORY FOR WOMEN

BLAZER

	SINGLE-BREASTED
WOOL/BLEND	
TWEED/HERRINGBONE	
CORDUROY	
SILK/BLEND	
COTTON/BLEND	
LINEN/BLEND	

SKIRT/SUIT SKIRT

	STRAIGHT	GORED/ A-LINE	PLEATED	SLIGHTLY GATHERED
WOOL/BLEND				
TWEED/HERRINGBONE				
CORDUROY				
SILK/BLEND				
COTTON/BLEND				
LINEN/BLEND				
SYNTHETIC				

JACKET/SUIT JACKET

	SINGLE-BREASTED	DOUBLE-BREASTED	VEST
WOOL/BLEND			
TWEED/HERRINGBONE			
CORDUROY			
SILK/BLEND			
COTTON/BLEND			
LINEN/BLEND			
CREPE			
SYNTHETIC			

TROUSERS (PANTS)

	TAILORED	CASUAL
WOOL/BLEND		
TWEED/HERRINGBONE		
CORDUROY		
COTTON/BLEND		
LINEN/BLEND		
DENIM		
SYNTHETIC		

COLOR GUIDE

B-BURGUNDY
BK-BLACK
BL-BLUE
BR-BROWN
CB-CREAM/BEIGE
DB-DENIM BLUE
G-GRAY
GR-GREEN
K-KHAKI
L-LAVENDER
M-MAUVE
N-NAVY
OR-ORANGE/RUST
P-PURPLE
PK-PINK
R-RED
W-WHITE
Y-YELLOW

DRESS

	SOLID	FOULARD	PATTERN	STRIPE
WOOL/BLEND				
SILK/BLEND				
COTTON/BLEND				
LINEN/BLEND				
SYNTHETIC				

BLOUSE

	SOLID	FOULARD	PATTERN	STRIPE
POLY/SYNTHETIC				
SILK/BLEND				
COTTON/BLEND				

SWEATER

	PULLOVER	CARDIGAN	SWEATER VEST
WOOL/BLEND			
CASHMERE			
SYNTHETIC			

EVENING WEAR

	DRESS	BLOUSE	JACKET	LONG SKIRT	PANTS	CAMISOLE
SILK						
SATIN						
SYNTHETIC						
GEORGETTE						
VELVET						
CREPE						

COAT

	RAIN	WINTER	CASUAL
WOOL/BLEND			
COTTON/BLEND			

HANDBAG

DAYTIME			
EVENING			
BRIEFCASE			

SCARVES

SOLID	
FOULARD	
STRIPE	
PATTERN	

SHOES

PUMPS	
SANDALS	
BOOTS	
METALLIC	

BELTS

LEATHER/SKIN	
SILK/CORD	
STRIPE	
CANVAS/ROPE	
METALLIC	

HOSIERY

NEUTRAL	
OYSTER	
GRAY	
BLACK	

WARDROBE INVENTORY FOR MEN

SUIT—SOLID COLOR

WOOL/BLEND
COTTON/BLEND
LINEN/BLEND
OTHER

SUIT—PIN-STRIPED

WOOL/BLEND
COTTON/BLEND
OTHER

SUIT—PLAID, TWEED, OR HERRINGBONE

WOOL/BLEND
COTTON/BLEND
OTHER

SHIRT—REGULAR COLLAR

SOLID
PIN-STRIPED
COLOR ON COLOR
PATTERNED

SHIRT—BUTTON-DOWN

SOLID
PIN-STRIPED
COLOR ON COLOR
PATTERNED

TIES

FOULARD
POLKA DOT
SOLID
STRIPED
PATTERN

BLAZER—SOLID COLOR

WOOL/BLEND
LINEN/BLEND
COTTON/BLEND
SILK/BLEND
CORDUROY

BLAZER—PLAID, TWEED, OR HERRINGBONE

WOOL/BLEND
COTTON/BLEND
OTHER

TROUSERS

DRESSY
CASUAL

SWEATERS

PULLOVER
CARDIGAN
VEST

COAT

TOPCOAT
CASUAL

SHOES—LEATHER

OXFORDS
SLIP-ONS
WING TIPS

BELT—LEATHER

DRESSY
CASUAL

SOCKS

DRESSY
CASUAL

COLOR GUIDE
B-BURGUNDY
BK-BLACK
BL-BLUE
BR-BROWN
C-CAMEL
OR BEIGE
DB-DENIM BLUE
G-GRAY
GR-GREEN
N-NAVY
P-PURPLE
PK-PINK
R-RED
W-WHITE
Y-YELLOW